POETRY

Lyrical Ballads

WILLIAM WORDSWORTH

AND

SAMUEL TAYLOR COLERIDGE

WILLIAM WORDSWORTH (1770–1850)
SAMUEL TAYLOR COLERIDGE (1772–1834)

Lyrical Ballads first published 1798

WILLIAM WORDSWORTH

AND

SAMUEL TAYLOR COLERIDGE

Lyrical Ballads
with a few other poems

with a note on the Text by
Michael Schmidt

PENGUIN BOOKS

PENGUIN BOOKS

Published by the Penguin Group
Penguin Books Ltd, 80 Strand, London WC2R 0RL, England
Penguin Putnam Inc., 375 Hudson Street, New York, New York 10014, USA
Penguin Books Australia Ltd, 250 Camberwell Road, Camberwell, Victoria 3124, Australia
Penguin Books Canada Ltd, 10 Alcorn Avenue, Toronto, Ontario, Canada M4V 3B2
Penguin Books India (P) Ltd, 11 Community Centre, Panchsheel Park, New Delhi – 110 017, India
Penguin Books (NZ) Ltd, Cnr Rosedale and Airborne Roads, Albany, Auckland, New Zealand
Penguin Books (South Africa) (Pty) Ltd, 24 Sturdee Avenue, Rosebank 2196, South Africa

Penguin Books Ltd, Registered Offices: 80 Strand, London WC2R 0RL, England

www.penguin.com

Published in Penguin Books 1999
9

The front cover shows a detail from *Slavers Throwing Overboard
the Dead and Dying – Typhoon Coming On*, 1841, by J. M. W. Turner in the
Museum of Fine Arts, Boston (photo: Corbis)

Set in 11/14 pt PostScript Monotype Baskerville
Typeset by Rowland Phototypesetting Ltd, Bury St Edmunds, Suffolk
Printed in England by Clays Ltd, St Ives plc

ADVERTISEMENT

It is the honourable characteristic of Poetry that its materials are to be found in every subject which can interest the human mind. The evidence of this fact is to be sought, not in the writings of Critics, but in those of Poets themselves.

The majority of the following poems are to be considered as experiments. They were written chiefly with a view to ascertain how far the language of conversation in the middle and lower classes of society is adapted to the purposes of poetic pleasure. Readers accustomed to the gaudiness and inane phraseology of many modern writers, if they persist in reading this book to its conclusion, will perhaps frequently have to struggle with feelings of strangeness and aukwardness: they will look round for poetry, and will be induced to enquire by what species of courtesy these attempts can be permitted to assume that title. It is desirable that such readers, for their own sakes, should not suffer the solitary word Poetry, a word of very disputed meaning, to stand in the way of their gratification; but that, while they are perusing this book, they should ask themselves if it contains a natural delineation of human passions, human characters, and human incidents; and if the answer be favorable to the author's wishes, that they should consent to be pleased in spite of that most dreadful enemy to our pleasures, our own pre-established codes of decision.

Readers of superior judgment may disapprove of the style in which many of these pieces are executed; it must be expected that many lines and phrases will not exactly suit their taste. It will perhaps appear to them, that wishing to avoid the prevalent fault of the day, the author has sometimes descended too low, and that many of his expressions are too familiar, and not of sufficient dignity. It is apprehended, that the more conversant the reader is with our elder writers, and with those in modern times who have been the most successful in painting manners and passions, the fewer complaints of this kind will he have to make.

An accurate taste in poetry, and in all the other arts, Sir Joshua Reynolds has observed, is an acquired talent, which can only be produced by severe thought, and a long continued intercourse with the best models of composition. This is mentioned not with so ridiculous a purpose as to prevent the most inexperienced reader from judging for himself; but merely to temper the rashness of decision, and to suggest that if poetry be a subject on which much time has not been bestowed, the judgment may be erroneous, and that in many cases it necessarily will be so.

The tale of Goody Blake and Harry Gill is founded on a well-authenticated fact which happened in Warwickshire. Of the other poems in the collection, it may be proper to say that they are either absolute inventions of the author, or facts which took place within his personal observation or that of his friends. The poem of the Thorn, as the reader will soon discover, is not supposed to be spoken in the author's own person: the character of the loquacious narrator will sufficiently shew itself in the course of the story. The Rime of the Ancyent Marinere was professedly written in imitation of the *style*, as well as of the spirit of the elder poets; but with a few exceptions, the Author believes that the language adopted in it has been equally intelligible for these three last centuries. The lines entitled Expostulation and Reply, and those which follow, arose out of conversation with a friend who was somewhat unreasonably attached to modern books of moral philosophy.

Listen, Stranger! Storm and Wind,
    A Wind and Tempest strong!
For days and weeks it play'd us freaks –
    Like Chaff we drove along.

Listen, Stranger! Mist and Snow,
    And it grew wond'rous cauld:
And Ice mast-high came floating by
    As green as Emerauld.

And thro' the drifts the snowy clifts
    Did send a dismal sheen;
Ne shapes of men ne beasts we ken –
    The Ice was all between.

The Ice was here, the Ice was there,
    The Ice was all around:
It crack'd and growl'd, and roar'd and howl'd –
    Like noises of a swound.

At length did cross an Albatross,
    Thorough the Fog it came;
And an it were a Christian Soul,
    We hail'd it in God's name.

The Marineres gave it biscuit-worms,
    And round and round it flew:
The Ice did split with a Thunder-fit;
    The Helmsman steer'd us thro'.

And a good south wind sprung up behind,
    The Albatross did follow;
And every day for food or play
    Came to the Marinere's hollo!

In mist or cloud on mast or shroud
    It perch'd for vespers nine,
Whiles all the night thro' fog-smoke white
    Glimmer'd the white moon-shine.

'God save thee, ancyent Marinere!
    'From the fiends that plague thee thus –
'Why look'st thou so?' – with my cross bow
    I shot the Albatross.

II

The Sun came up upon the right,
    Out of the Sea came he;
And broad as a weft upon the left
    Went down into the Sea.

And the good south wind still blew behind,
    But no sweet Bird did follow
Ne any day for food or play
    Came to the Marinere's hollo!

And I had done an hellish thing
    And it would work 'em woe:
For all averr'd, I had kill'd the Bird
    That made the Breeze to blow.

Ne dim ne red, like God's own head,
    The glorious Sun uprist:
Then all averr'd, I had kill'd the Bird
    That brought the fog and mist.
'Twas right, said they, such birds to slay
    That bring the fog and mist.

The breezes blew, the white foam flew,
    The furrow follow'd free:
We were the first that ever burst
    Into that silent Sea.

Down dropt the breeze, the Sails dropt down,
    'Twas sad as sad could be
And we did speak only to break
    The silence of the Sea.

All in a hot and copper sky
    The bloody sun at noon,
Right up above the mast did stand,
    No bigger than the moon.

Day after day, day after day,
    We stuck, ne breath ne motion,
As idle as a painted Ship
    Upon a painted Ocean.

Water, water, every where
    And all the boards did shrink;
Water, water, every where
    Ne any drop to drink.

The very deeps did rot: O Christ!
    That ever this should be!
Yea, slimy things did crawl with legs
    Upon the slimy Sea.

About, about, in reel and rout
    The Death-fires danc'd at night;
The water, like a witch's oils,
    Burnt green and blue and white.

And some in dreams assured were
    Of the Spirit that plagued us so:
Nine fathom deep he had follow'd us
    From the Land of Mist and Snow.

And every tongue thro' utter drouth
    Was wither'd at the root;
We could not speak no more than if
    We had been choked with soot.

Ah wel-a-day! what evil looks
    Had I from old and young;
Instead of the Cross the Albatross
    About my neck was hung.

III

I saw a something in the Sky
    No bigger than my fist;
At first it seem'd a little speck
    And then it seem'd a mist:
It mov'd and mov'd, and took at last
    A certain shape, I wist.

A speck, a mist, a shape, I wist!
    And still it ner'd and ner'd;
And, an it dodg'd a water-sprite,
    It plung'd and tack'd and veer'd.

With throat unslack'd, with black lips bak'd
    Ne could we laugh, ne wail:
Then while thro' drouth all dumb they stood
I bit my arm and suck'd the blood
    And cry'd, A sail! a sail!

With throat unslack'd, with black lips bak'd
    Agape they hear'd me call:
Gramercy! they for joy did grin
And all at once their breath drew in
    As they were drinking all.

She doth not tack from side to side –
    Hither to work us weal
Withouten wind, withouten tide
    She steddies with upright keel.

The western wave was all a flame,
    The day was well nigh done!
Almost upon the western wave
    Rested the broad bright Sun;
When that strange shape drove suddenly
    Betwixt us and the Sun.

And strait the Sun was fleck'd with bars
    (Heaven's mother send us grace)
As if thro' a dungeon grate he peer'd
    With broad and burning face.

Alas! (thought I, and my heart beat loud)
    How fast she neres and neres!
Are those *her* Sails that glance in the Sun
    Like restless gossameres?

Are these *her* naked ribs, which fleck'd
    The sun that did behind them peer?
And are these two all, all the crew,
    That woman and her fleshless Pheere?

His bones were black with many a crack,
　　All black and bare, I ween;
Jet-black and bare, save where with rust
Of mouldy damps and charnel crust
　　They're patch'd with purple and green.

Her lips are red, *her* looks are free,
　　Her locks are yellow as gold:
Her skin is as white as leprosy,
And she is far liker Death than he;
　　Her flesh makes the still air cold.

The naked Hulk alongside came
　　And the Twain were playing dice;
'The Game is done! I've won, I've won!'
　　Quoth she, and whistled thrice.

A gust of wind sterte up behind
　　And whistled thro' his bones;
Thro' the holes of his eyes and the hole of his mouth
　　Half-whistles and half-groans.

With never a whisper in the Sea
　　Off darts the Spectre-ship;
While clombe above the Eastern bar
The horned Moon, with one bright Star
　　Almost atween the tips.

One after one by the horned Moon
　　(Listen, O Stranger! to me)
Each turn'd his face with a ghastly pang
　　And curs'd me with his ee.

Four times fifty living men,
   With never a sigh or groan,
With heavy thump, a lifeless lump
   They dropp'd down one by one.

Their souls did from their bodies fly, –
   They fled to bliss or woe;
And every soul it pass'd me by,
   Like the whiz of my Cross-bow.

IV

'I fear thee, ancyent Marinere!
   'I fear thy skinny hand;
'And thou art long and lank and brown
   'As is the ribb'd Sea-sand.

'I fear thee and thy glittering eye
   'And thy skinny hand so brown –
Fear not, fear not, thou wedding guest!
   This body dropt not down.

Alone, alone, all all alone
   Alone on the wide wide Sea;
And Christ would take no pity on
   My soul in agony.

The many men so beautiful,
   And they all dead did lie!
And a million million slimy things
   Liv'd on – and so did I.

I look'd upon the rotting Sea,
   And drew my eyes away;
I look'd upon the eldritch deck,
   And there the dead men lay.

I look'd to Heaven, and try'd to pray;
   But or ever a prayer had gusht,
A wicked whisper came and made
   My heart as dry as dust.

I clos'd my lids and kept them close,
   Till the balls like pulses beat;
For the sky and the sea, and the sea and the sky
Lay like a load on my weary eye,
   And the dead were at my feet.

The cold sweat melted from their limbs,
   Ne rot, ne reek did they;
The look with which they look'd on me,
   Had never pass'd away.

An orphan's curse would drag to Hell
   A spirit from on high:
But O! more horrible than that
   Is the curse in a dead man's eye!
Seven days, seven nights I saw that curse,
   And yet I could not die.

The moving Moon went up the sky
   And no where did abide:
Softly she was going up ·
   And a star or two beside

Her beams bemock'd the sultry main
  Like morning frosts yspread;
But where the ship's huge shadow lay,
The charmed water burnt alway
  A still and awful red.

Beyond the shadow of the ship
  I watch'd the water-snakes:
They mov'd in tracks of shining white;
And when they rear'd, the elfish light
  Fell off in hoary flakes.

Within the shadow of the ship
  I watch'd their rich attire:
Blue, glossy green, and velvet black
They coil'd and swam; and every track
  Was a flash of golden fire.

O happy living things! no tongue
  Their beauty might declare:
A spring of love gusht from my heart,
  And I bless'd them unaware!
Sure my kind saint took pity on me,
  And I bless'd them unaware.

The self-same moment I could pray;
  And from my neck so free
The Albatross fell off, and sank
  Like lead into the sea.

V

O sleep, it is a gentle thing
  Belov'd from pole to pole!
To Mary-queen the praise be yeven
She sent the gentle sleep from heaven
  That slid into my soul.

The silly buckets on the deck
  That had so long remain'd,
I dreamt that they were fill'd with dew
  And when I awoke it rain'd.

My lips were wet, my throat was cold,
  My garments all were dank;
Sure I had drunken in my dreams
  And still my body drank.

I mov'd and could not feel my limbs,
  I was so light, almost
I thought that I had died in sleep,
  And was a blessed Ghost.

The roaring wind! it roar'd far off,
  It did not come anear;
But with its sound it shook the sails
  That were so thin and sere.

The upper air bursts into life,
  And a hundred fire-flags sheen
To and fro they are hurried about;
And to and fro, and in and out
  The stars dance on between.

The coming wind doth roar more loud;
   The sails do sigh, like sedge:
The rain pours down from one black cloud
   And the Moon is at its edge.

Hark! hark! the thick black cloud is cleft,
   And the Moon is at its side:
Like waters shot from some high crag,
The lightning falls with never a jag
   A river steep and wide.

The strong wind reach'd the ship: it roar'd
   And dropp'd down, like a stone!
Beneath the lightning and the moon
   The dead men gave a groan.

They groan'd, they stirr'd, they all uprose,
   Ne spake, ne mov'd their eyes:
It had been strange, even in a dream
   To have seen those dead men rise.

The helmsman steerd, the ship mov'd on;
   Yet never a breeze up-blew;
The Marineres all 'gan work the ropes,
   Where they were wont to do:
They rais'd their limbs like lifeless tools –
   We were a ghastly crew.

The body of my brother's son
   Stood by me knee to knee:
The body and I pull'd at one rope,
   But he said nought to me –
And I quak'd to think of my own voice
   How frightful it would be!

The day-light dawn'd – they dropp'd their arms,
    And cluster'd round the mast:
Sweet sounds rose slowly thro' their mouths
    And from their bodies pass'd.

Around, around, flew each sweet sound,
    Then darted to the sun:
Slowly the sounds came back again
    Now mix'd, now one by one.

Sometimes a dropping from the sky
    I heard the Lavrock sing;
Sometimes all little birds that are
How they seem'd to fill the sea and air
    With their sweet jargoning,

And now 'twas like all instruments,
    Now like a lonely flute;
And now it is an angel's song
    That makes the heavens be mute.

It ceas'd: yet still the sails made on
    A pleasant noise till noon,
A noise like of a hidden brook
    In the leafy month of June,
That to the sleeping woods all night
    Singeth a quiet tune.

Listen, O listen, thou Wedding-guest!
    'Marinere! thou hast thy will:
'For that, which comes out of thine eye, doth make
    'My body and soul to be still.'

Never sadder tale was told
    To a man of woman born:
Sadder and wiser thou wedding-guest!
    Thou'lt rise to morrow morn.

Never sadder tale was heard
    By a man of woman born:
The Marineres all return'd to work
    As silent as beforne.

The Marineres all 'gan pull the ropes,
    But look at me they n'old:
Thought I, I am as thin as air –
    They cannot me behold.

Till noon we silently sail'd on
    Yet never a breeze did breathe:
Slowly and smoothly went the ship
    Mov'd onward from beneath.

Under the keel nine fathom deep
    From the land of mist and snow
The spirit slid: and it was He
    That made the Ship to go.
The sails at noon left off their tune
    And the Ship stood still also.

The sun right up above the mast
    Had fix'd her to the ocean:
But in a minute she 'gan stir
    With a short uneasy motion –
Backwards and forwards half her length
    With a short uneasy motion.

Then, like a pawing horse let go,
   She made a sudden bound:
It flung the blood into my head,
   And I fell into a swound.

How long in that same fit I lay,
   I have not to declare;
But ere my living life return'd,
I heard and in my soul discern'd
   Two voices in the air,

'Is it he?' quoth one, 'Is this the man?
   'By him who died on cross,
'With his cruel bow he lay'd full low
   'The harmless Albatross.

'The spirit who 'bideth by himself
   'In the land of mist and snow,
'He lov'd the bird that lov'd the man
   'Who shot him with his bow.

The other was a softer voice,
   As soft as honey-dew:
Quoth he the man hath penance done,
   And penance more will do.

VI

FIRST VOICE

'But tell me, tell me! speak again,
   'Thy soft response renewing –
'What makes that ship drive on so fast?
   'What is the Ocean doing?

SECOND VOICE

'Still as a Slave before his Lord,
  'The Ocean hath no blast:
'His great bright eye most silently
  'Up to the moon is cast –

'If he may know which way to go,
  'For she guides him smooth or grim.
'See, brother, see! how graciously
  'She looketh down on him.

FIRST VOICE

'But why drives on that ship so fast
  'Withouten wave or wind?

SECOND VOICE

'The air is cut away before,
  'And closes from behind.

'Fly, brother, fly! more high, more high,
  'Or we shall be belated:
'For slow and slow that ship will go,
  'When the Marinere's trance is abated.'

I woke, and we were sailing on
  As in a gentle weather:
'Twas night, calm night, the moon was high;
  The dead men stood together.

All stood together on the deck,
    For a charnel-dungeon fitter:
All fix'd on me their stony eyes
    That in the moon did glitter.

The pang, the curse, with which they died,
    Had never pass'd away:
I could not draw my een from theirs
    Ne turn them up to pray.

And in its time the spell was snapt,
    And I could move my een:
I look'd far-forth, but little saw
    Of what might else be seen.

Like one, that on a lonely road
    Doth walk in fear and dread,
And having once turn'd round, walks on
    And turns no more his head:
Because he knows, a frightful fiend
    Doth close behind him tread.

But soon there breath'd a wind on me,
    Ne sound ne motion made:
Its path was not upon the sea
    In ripple or in shade.

It rais'd my hair, it fann'd my cheek,
    Like a meadow-gale of spring –
It mingled strangely with my fears,
    Yet it felt like a welcoming.

Swiftly, swiftly flew the ship,
  Yet she sail'd softly too:
Sweetly, sweetly blew the breeze –
  On me alone it blew.

  O dream of joy! is this indeed
    The light-house top I see?
  Is this the Hill? Is this the Kirk?
    Is this mine own countrée?

  We drifted o'er the Harbour-bar,
    And I with sobs did pray –
  'O let me be awake, my God!
    'Or let me sleep alway!'

  The harbour-bay was clear as glass,
    So smoothly it was strewn!
  And on the bay the moon light lay,
    And the shadow of the moon.

  The moonlight bay was white all o'er,
    Till rising from the same,
  Full many shapes, that shadows were,
    Like as of torches came.

  A little distance from the prow
    Those dark-red shadows were;
  But soon I saw that my own flesh
    Was red as in a glare.

  I turn'd my head in fear and dread,
    And by the holy rood,
  The bodies had advanc'd, and now
    Before the mast they stood.

They lifted up their stiff right arms,
　　They held them strait and tight;
And each right-arm burnt like a torch,
　　A torch that's borne upright.
Their stony eye-balls glitter'd on
　　In the red and smoky light.

I pray'd and turn'd my head away
　　Forth looking as before.
There was no breeze upon the bay,
　　No wave against the shore.

The rock shone bright, the kirk no less
　　That stands above the rock:
The moonlight steep'd in silentness
　　The steady weathercock.

And the bay was white with silent light,
　　Till rising from the same
Full many shapes, that shadows were,
　　In crimson colours came.

A little distance from the prow
　　Those crimson shadows were:
I turn'd my eyes upon the deck –
　　O Christ! what saw I there?

Each corse lay flat, lifeless and flat;
　　And by the Holy rood
A man all light, a seraph-man,
　　On every corse there stood.

This seraph-band, each wav'd his hand:
　　It was a heavenly sight:
They stood as signals to the land,
　　Each one a lovely light:

This seraph-band, each wav'd his hand,
　　No voice did they impart –
No voice; but O! the silence sank,
　　Like music on my heart.

Eftsones I heard the dash of oars,
　　I heard the pilot's cheer:
My head was turn'd perforce away
　　And I saw a boat appear.

Then vanish'd all the lovely lights;
　　The bodies rose anew:
With silent pace, each to his place,
　　Came back the ghastly crew.
The wind, that shade nor motion made,
　　On me alone it blew.

The pilot, and the pilot's boy
　　I heard them coming fast:
Dear Lord in Heaven! it was a joy,
　　The dead men could not blast.

I saw a third – I heard his voice:
　　It is the Hermit good!
He singeth loud his godly hymns
　　That he makes in the wood.
He'll shrieve my soul, he'll wash away
　　The Albatross's blood.

VII

This Hermit good lives in that wood
   Which slopes down to the Sea.
How loudly his sweet voice he rears!
He loves to talk with Marineres
   That come from a far Contrée.

He kneels at morn and noon and eve –
   He hath a cushion plump:
It is the moss, that wholly hides
   The rotted old Oak-stump.

The Skiff-boat ne'rd: I heard them talk,
   'Why, this is strange, I trow!
'Where are those lights so many and fair
   'That signal made but now?

'Strange, by my faith! the Hermit said –
   'And they answer'd not our cheer.
'The planks look warp'd, and see those sails
   'How thin they are and sere!
'I never saw aught like to them
   'Unless perchance it were

'The skeletons of leaves that lag
   'My forest brook along:
'When the Ivy-tod is heavy with snow,
'And the Owlet whoops to the wolf below
   'That eats the she-wolf's young.

'Dear Lord! it has a fiendish look –
   (The Pilot made reply)
'I am a-fear'd. – 'Push on, push on!
   'Said the Hermit cheerily.

The Boat came closer to the Ship,
    But I ne spake ne stirr'd!
The Boat came close beneath the Ship,
    And strait a sound was heard!

Under the water it rumbled on,
    Still louder and more dread:
It reach'd the Ship, it split the bay;
    The Ship went down like lead.

Stunn'd by that loud and dreadful sound,
    Which sky and ocean smote:
Like one that hath been seven days drown'd
    My body lay afloat:
But, swift as dreams, myself I found
    Within the Pilot's boat.

Upon the whirl, where sank the Ship,
    The boat spun round and round:
And all was still, save that the hill
    Was telling of the sound.

I mov'd my lips: the Pilot shriek'd
    And fell down in a fit.
The Holy Hermit rais'd his eyes
    And pray'd where he did sit.

I took the oars: the Pilot's boy,
    Who now doth crazy go,
Laugh'd loud and long, and all the while
    His eyes went to and fro,
'Ha! ha!' quoth he – 'full plain I see,
    'The devil knows how to row.'

And now all in mine own Countrée
    I stood on the firm land!
The Hermit stepp'd forth from the boat,
    And scarcely he could stand.

'O shrieve me, shrieve me, holy Man!
    The Hermit cross'd his brow –
'Say quick,' quoth he, 'I bid thee say
    'What manner man art thou?

Forthwith this frame of mine was wrench'd
    With a woeful agony,
Which forc'd me to begin my tale
    And then it left me free.

Since then at an uncertain hour,
    Now oftimes and now fewer,
That anguish comes and makes me tell
    My ghastly aventure.

I pass, like night, from land to land;
    I have strange power of speech;
The moment that his face I see
I know the man that must hear me;
    To him my tale I teach.

What loud uproar bursts from that door!
    The Wedding-guests are there;
But in the Garden-bower the Bride
    And Bride-maids singing are:
And hark the little Vesper-bell
    Which biddeth me to prayer.

O Wedding-guest! this soul hath been
  Alone on a wide wide sea:
So lonely 'twas, that God himself
  Scarce seemed there to be.

O sweeter than the Marriage-feast,
  'Tis sweeter far to me
To walk together to the Kirk
  With a goodly company.

To walk together to the Kirk
  And all together pray,
While each to his great father bends,
Old men, and babes, and loving friends,
  And Youths, and Maidens gay.

Farewell, farewell! but this I tell
  To thee, thou wedding-guest!
He prayeth well who loveth well
  Both man and bird and beast.

He prayeth best who loveth best,
  All things both great and small:
For the dear God, who loveth us,
  He made and loveth all.

The Marinere, whose eye is bright,
  Whose beard with age is hoar,
Is gone; and now the wedding-guest
  Turn'd from the bridegroom's door.

He went, like one that hath been stunn'd
  And is of sense forlorn:
A sadder and a wiser man
  He rose the morrow morn.

The Foster-Mother's Tale

A DRAMATIC FRAGMENT

FOSTER-MOTHER

I never saw the man whom you describe.

MARIA

'Tis strange! he spake of you familiarly
As mine and Albert's common Foster-mother.

FOSTER-MOTHER

Now blessings on the man, who'er he be,
That joined your names with mine! O my sweet lady,
As often as I think of those dear times
When you two little ones would stand at eve
On each side of my chair, and make me learn
All you had learnt in the day; and how to talk
In gentle phrase, then bid me sing to you –
'Tis more like heaven to come than what *has* been.

MARIA

O my dear Mother! this strange man has left me
Troubled with wilder fancies, than the moon
Breeds in the love-sick maid who gazes at it,
Till lost in inward vision, with wet eye
She gazes idly! – But that entrance, Mother!

FOSTER-MOTHER

Can no one hear? It is a perilous tale!

MARIA

No one.

FOSTER-MOTHER

My husband's father told it me,
Poor old Leoni! – Angels rest his soul!
He was a woodman, and could fell and saw
With lusty arm. You know that huge round beam
Which props the hanging wall of the old chapel?
Beneath that tree, while yet it was a tree
He found a baby wrapt in mosses, lined
With thistle-beards, and such small locks of wool
As hang on brambles. Well, he brought him home,
And reared him at the then Lord Velez' cost.
And so the babe grew up a pretty boy,
A pretty boy, but most unteachable –
And never learnt a prayer, nor told a bead,
But knew the names of birds, and mocked their notes,
And whistled, as he were a bird himself:
And all the autumn 'twas his only play
To get the seeds of wild flowers, and to plant them
With earth and water, on the stumps of trees.
A Friar, who gathered simples in the wood,
A grey-haired man – he loved this little boy,
The boy loved him – and, when the Friar taught him,
He soon could write with the pen: and from that time,
Lived chiefly at the Convent or the Castle.
So he became a very learned youth.
But Oh! poor wretch! – he read, and read, and read,
'Till his brain turned – and ere his twentieth year,
He had unlawful thoughts of many things:
And though he prayed, he never loved to pray
With holy men, nor in a holy place –
But yet his speech, it was so soft and sweet,
The late Lord Velez ne'er was wearied with him.
And once, as by the north side of the Chapel
They stood together, chained in deep discourse,
The earth heaved under them with such a groan,

That the wall tottered, and had well-nigh fallen
Right on their heads. My Lord was sorely frightened;
A fever seized him, and he made confession
Of all the heretical and lawless talk
Which brought this judgment: so the youth was seized
And cast into that hole. My husband's father
Sobbed like a child – it almost broke his heart:
And once as he was working in the cellar,
He heard a voice distinctly; 'twas the youth's,
Who sung a doleful song about green fields,
How sweet it were on lake or wild savannah,
To hunt for food, and be a naked man,
And wander up and down at liberty.
He always doted on the youth, and now
His love grew desperate; and defying death,
He made that cunning entrance I described:
And the young man escaped.

MARIA

                'Tis a sweet tale:
Such as would lull a listening child to sleep,
His rosy face besoiled with unwiped tears. –
And what became of him?

FOSTER-MOTHER

                He went on ship-board
With those bold voyagers, who made discovery
Of golden lands. Leoni's younger brother
Went likewise, and when he returned to Spain,
He told Leoni, that the poor mad youth,
Soon after they arrived in that new world,
In spite of his dissuasion, seized a boat,
And all alone, set sail by silent moonlight

Up a great river, great as any sea,
And ne'er was heard of more: but 'tis supposed,
He lived and died among the savage men.

Lines left upon a Seat in a Yew-tree
WHICH STANDS NEAR THE LAKE OF ESTHWAITE, ON A DESOLATE PART OF THE SHORE, YET COMMANDING A BEAUTIFUL PROSPECT

– Nay, Traveller! rest. This lonely yew-tree stands
Far from all human dwelling: what if here
No sparkling rivulets spread the verdant herb;
What if these barren boughs the bee not loves;
Yet, if the wind breathe soft, the curling waves,
That break against the shore, shall lull thy mind
By one soft impulse saved from vacancy.

————————Who he was
That piled these stones, and with the mossy sod
First covered o'er, and taught this aged tree,
Now wild, to bend its arms in circling shade,
I well remember. – He was one who own'd
No common soul. In youth, by genius nurs'd,
And big with lofty views, he to the world
Went forth, pure in his heart, against the taint
Of dissolute tongues, 'gainst jealousy, and hate,
And scorn, against all enemies prepared,
All but neglect: and so, his spirit damped
At once, with rash disdain he turned away,
And with the food of pride sustained his soul
In solitude. – Stranger! these gloomy boughs
Had charms for him; and here he loved to sit,
His only visitants a straggling sheep,
The stone-chat, or the glancing sand-piper;
And on these barren rocks, with juniper,
And heath, and thistle, thinly sprinkled o'er,
Fixing his downward eye, he many an hour
A morbid pleasure nourished, tracing here

An emblem of his own unfruitful life:
And lifting up his head, he then would gaze
On the more distant scene; how lovely 'tis
Thou seest, and he would gaze till it became
Far lovelier, and his heart could not sustain
The beauty still more beauteous. Nor, that time,
Would he forget those beings, to whose minds,
Warm from the labours of benevolence,
The world, and man himself, appeared a scene
Of kindred loveliness: then he would sigh
With mournful joy, to think that others felt
What he must never feel: and so, lost man!
On visionary views would fancy feed,
Till his eye streamed with tears. In this deep vale
He died, this seat his only monument.

If thou be one whose heart the holy forms
Of young imagination have kept pure,
Stranger! henceforth be warned; and know, that pride,
Howe'er disguised in its own majesty,
Is littleness; that he, who feels contempt
For any living thing, hath faculties
Which he has never used; that thought with him
Is in its infancy. The man, whose eye
Is ever on himself, doth look on one,
The least of nature's works, one who might move
The wise man to that scorn which wisdom holds
Unlawful, ever. O, be wiser thou!
Instructed that true knowledge leads to love,
True dignity abides with him alone
Who, in the silent hour of inward thought,
Can still suspect, and still revere himself,
In lowliness of heart.

The Nightingale

A CONVERSATIONAL POEM, WRITTEN IN APRIL 1798

No cloud, no relique of the sunken day
Distinguishes the West, no long thin slip
Of sullen Light, no obscure trembling hues.
Come, we will rest on this old mossy Bridge!
You see the glimmer of the stream beneath.
But hear no murmuring: it flows silently
O'er its soft bed of verdure. All is still,
A balmy night! and tho' the stars be dim,
Yet let us think upon the vernal showers
That gladden the green earth, and we shall find
A pleasure in the dimness of the stars.
And hark! the Nightingale begins its song,
'Most musical, most melancholy'* Bird!
A melancholy Bird? O idle thought!
In nature there is nothing melancholy.
– But some night-wandering Man, whose
            heart was pierc'd
With the remembrance of a grievous wrong,
Or slow distemper or neglected love,
(And so, poor Wretch! fill'd all things with himself
And made all gentle sounds tell back the tale
Of his own sorrows) he and such as he
First nam'd these notes a melancholy strain;
And many a poet echoes the conceit,
Poet, who hath been building up the rhyme

---

* 'Most musical, most melancholy.' This passage in Milton possesses an excellence
far superior to that of mere description: it is spoken in the character of the
melancholy Man, and has therefore a dramatic propriety. The Author makes
this remark, to rescue himself from the charge of having alluded with levity
to a line in Milton: a charge than which none could be more painful to him,
except perhaps that of having ridiculed his Bible.

When he had better far have stretch'd his limbs
Beside a brook in mossy forest-dell
By sun or moonlight, to the influxes
Of shapes and sounds and shifting elements
Surrendering his whole spirit, of his song
And of his fame forgetful! so his fame
Should share in nature's immortality,
A venerable thing! and so his song
Should make all nature lovelier, and itself
Be lov'd, like nature! – But 'twill not be so;
And youths and maidens most poetical
Who lose the deep'ning twilights of the spring
In ball-rooms and hot theatres, they still
Full of meek sympathy must heave their sighs
O'er Philomela's pity-pleading strains.
My Friend, and my Friend's Sister! we have learnt
A different lore: we may not thus profane
Nature's sweet voices always full of love
And joyance! 'Tis the merry Nightingale
That crowds, and hurries, and precipitates
With fast thick warble his delicious notes,
As he were fearful, that an April night
Would be too short for him to utter forth
His love-chant, and disburthen his full soul
Of all its music! And I know a grove
Of large extent, hard by a castle huge
Which the great lord inhabits not: and so
This grove is wild with tangling underwood,
And the trim walks are broken up, and grass,
Thin grass and king-cups grow within the paths.
But never elsewhere in one place I knew
So many Nightingales: and far and near
In wood and thicket over the wide grove
They answer and provoke each other's songs –
With skirmish and capricious passagings,

And murmurs musical and swift jug jug
And one low piping sound more sweet than all –
Stirring the air with such an harmony,
That should you close your eyes, you might almost
Forget it was not day! On moonlight bushes,
Whose dewy leafits are but half disclos'd,
You may perchance behold them on the twigs,
Their bright, bright eyes, their eyes both bright and full,
Glistning, while many a glow-worm in the shade
Lights up her love-torch.

                      A most gentle maid
Who dwelleth in her hospitable home
Hard by the Castle, and at latest eve,
(Even like a Lady vow'd and dedicate
To something more than nature in the grove)
Glides thro' the pathways; she knows all their notes,
That gentle Maid! and oft, a moment's space,
What time the moon was lost behind a cloud,
Hath heard a pause of silence: till the Moon
Emerging, hath awaken'd earth and sky
With one sensation, and those wakeful Birds
Have all burst forth in choral minstrelsy,
As if one quick and sudden Gale had swept
An hundred airy harps! And she hath watch'd
Many a Nightingale perch giddily
On blosmy twig still swinging from the breeze,
And to that motion tune his wanton song,
Like tipsy Joy that reels with tossing head.

Farewell, O Warbler! till to-morrow eve,
And you, my friends! farewell, a short farewell!
We have been loitering long and pleasantly,
And now for our dear homes. – That strain again!
Full fain it would delay me! – My dear Babe,

Who, capable of no articulate sound,
Mars all things with his imitative lisp,
How he would place his hand beside his ear,
His little hand, the small forefinger up,
And bid us listen! And I deem it wise
To make him Nature's playmate. He knows well
The evening star: and once when he awoke
In most distressful mood (some inward pain
Had made up that strange thing, an infant's dream)
I hurried with him to our orchard plot,
And he beholds the moon, and hush'd at once
Suspends his sobs, and laughs most silently,
While his fair eyes that swam with undropt tears
Did glitter in the yellow moon-beam! Well –
It is a father's tale. But if that Heaven
Should give me life, his childhood shall grow up
Familiar with these songs, that with the night
He may associate Joy! Once more farewell,
Sweet Nightingale! once more, my friends! farewell.

The Female Vagrant

By Derwent's side my Father's cottage stood,
(The Woman thus her artless story told)
One field, a flock, and what the neighbouring flood
Supplied, to him were more than mines of gold.
Light was my sleep; my days in transport roll'd:
With thoughtless joy I stretch'd along the shore
My father's nets, or watched, when from the fold
High o'er the cliffs I led my fleecy store,
A dizzy depth below! his boat and twinkling oar.

My father was a good and pious man,
An honest man by honest parents bred,
And I believe that, soon as I began
To lisp, he made me kneel beside my bed,
And in his hearing there my prayers I said:
And afterwards, by my good father taught,
I read, and loved the books in which I read;
For books in every neighbouring house I sought,
And nothing to my mind a sweeter pleasure brought.

Can I forget what charms did once adorn
My garden, stored with pease, and mint, and thyme,
And rose and lilly for the sabbath morn?
The sabbath bells, and their delightful chime;
The gambols and wild freaks at shearing time;
My hens's rich nest through long grass scarce espied;
The cowslip-gathering at May's dewy prime;
The swans, that, when I sought the water-side,
From far to meet me came, spreading their snowy pride.

The staff I yet remember which upbore
The bending body of my active sire;
His seat beneath the honeyed sycamore
When the bees hummed, and chair by winter fire;
When market-morning came, the neat attire
With which, though bent on haste, myself I deck'd;
My watchful dog, whose starts of furious ire,
When stranger passed, so often I have check'd;
The red-breast known for years, which at my casement
　　peck'd.

The suns of twenty summers danced along, –
Ah! little marked, how fast they rolled away:
Then rose a mansion proud our woods among,
And cottage after cottage owned its sway,
No joy to see a neighbouring house, or stray
Through pastures not his own, the master took;
My Father dared his greedy wish gainsay;
He loved his old hereditary nook,
And ill could I the thought of such sad parting brook.

But, when he had refused the proffered gold,
To cruel injuries he became a prey,
Sore-traversed in whate'er he bought and sold:
His troubles grew upon him day by day,
Till all his substance fell into decay.
His little range of water was denied;*
All but the bed where his old body lay,
All, all was seized, and weeping, side by side,
We sought a home where we uninjured might abide.

* Several of the Lakes in the north of England are let out to different
Fishermen, in parcels marked out by imaginary lines drawn from rock to
rock.

Can I forget that miserable hour,
When from the last hill-top, my sire surveyed,
Peering above the trees, the steeple tower,
That on his marriage-day sweet music made?
Till then he hoped his bones might there be laid,
Close by my mother in their native bowers:
Bidding me trust in God, he stood and prayed, –
I could not pray: – through tears that fell in showers,
Glimmer'd our dear-loved home, alas! no longer ours!

There was a youth whom I had loved so long,
That when I loved him not I cannot say.
'Mid the green mountains many and many a song
We two had sung, like little birds in May.
When we began to tire of childish play
We seemed still more and more to prize each other:
We talked of marriage and our marriage day;
And I in truth did love him like a brother,
For never could I hope to meet with such another.

His father said, that to a distant town
He must repair, to ply the artist's trade.
What tears of bitter grief till then unknown!
What tender vows our last sad kiss delayed!
To him we turned: – we had no other aid.
Like one revived, upon his neck I wept,
And her whom he had loved in joy, he said
He well could love in grief: his faith he kept;
And in a quiet home once more my father slept.

Four years each day with daily bread was blest,
By constant toil and constant prayer supplied.
Three lovely infants lay upon my breast;
And often, viewing their sweet smiles, I sighed,
And knew not why. My happy father died

When sad distress reduced the children's meal:
Thrice happy! that from him the grave did hide
The empty loom, cold hearth, and silent wheel,
And tears that flowed for ills which patience could not
heal.

'Twas a hard change, an evil time was come;
We had no hope, and no relief could gain.
But soon, with proud parade, the noisy drum
Beat round, to sweep the streets of want and pain.
My husband's arms now only served to strain
Me and his children hungering in his view:
In such dismay my prayers and tears were vain:
To join those miserable men he flew;
And now to the sea-coast, with numbers more, we drew.

There foul neglect for months and months we bore,
Nor yet the crowded fleet its anchor stirred.
Green fields before us and our native shore,
By fever, from polluted air incurred,
Ravage was made, for which no knell was heard.
Fondly we wished, and wished away, nor knew,
'Mid that long sickness, and those hopes deferr'd,
That happier days we never more must view:
The parting signal streamed, at last the land withdrew,

But from delay the summer calms were past.
On as we drove, the equinoctial deep
Ran mountains-high before the howling blast.
We gazed with terror on the gloomy sleep
Of them that perished in the whirlwind's sweep,
Untaught that soon such anguish must ensue,
Our hopes such harvest of affliction reap,
That we the mercy of the waves should rue.
We reached the western world, a poor, devoted crew.

Oh! dreadful price of being to resign
All that is dear *in* being! better far
In Want's most lonely cave till death to pine,
Unseen, unheard, unwatched by any star;
Or in the streets and walks where proud men are,
Better our dying bodies to obtrude,
Than dog-like, wading at the heels of war,
Protract a curst existence, with the brood
That lap (their very nourishment!) their brother's
    blood.

The pains and plagues that on our heads came down,
Disease and famine, agony and fear,
In wood or wilderness, in camp or town,
It would thy brain unsettle even to hear.
All perished – all, in one remorseless year,
Husband and children! one by one, by sword
And ravenous plague, all perished: every tear
Dried up, despairing, desolate, on board
A British ship I waked, as from a trance restored.

Peaceful as some immeasurable plain
By the first beams of dawning light impress'd,
In the calm sunshine slept the glittering main.
The very ocean has its hour of rest,
That comes not to the human mourner's breast.
Remote from man, and storms of mortal care,
A heavenly silence did the waves invest;
I looked and looked along the silent air,
Until it seemed to bring a joy to my despair.

Ah! how unlike those late terrific sleeps!
And groans, that rage of racking famine spoke,
Where looks inhuman dwelt on festering heaps!
The breathing pestilence that rose like smoke!

The shriek that from the distant battle broke!
The mine's dire earthquake, and the pallid host
Driven by the bomb's incessant thunder-stroke
To loathsome vaults, where heart-sick anguish toss'd,
Hope died, and fear itself in agony was lost!

Yet does that burst of woe congeal my frame,
When the dark streets appeared to heave and gape,
While like a sea the storming army came,
And Fire from Hell reared his gigantic shape,
And Murder, by the ghastly gleam, and Rape
Seized their joint prey, the mother and the child!
But from these crazing thoughts my brain, escape!
– For weeks the balmy air breathed soft and mild,
And on the gliding vessel Heaven and Ocean smiled.

Some mighty gulph of separation past,
I seemed transported to another world: –
A thought resigned with pain, when from the mast
The impatient mariner the sail unfurl'd,
And whistling, called the wind that hardly curled
The silent sea. From the sweet thoughts of home,
And from all hope I was forever hurled.
For me – farthest from earthly port to roam
Was best, could I but shun the spot where man might come.

And oft, robb'd of my perfect mind, I thought
At last my feet a resting-place had found:
Here will I weep in peace, (so fancy wrought,)
Roaming the illimitable waters round;
Here watch, of every human friend disowned,
All day, my ready tomb the ocean-flood –
To break my dream the vessel reached its bound:
And homeless near a thousand homes I stood,
And near a thousand tables pined, and wanted food.

By grief enfeebled was I turned adrift,
Helpless as sailor cast on desart rock;
Nor morsel to my mouth that day did lift,
Nor dared my hand at any door to knock.
I lay, where with his drowsy mates, the cock
From the cross timber of an out-house hung;
How dismal tolled, that night, the city clock!
At morn my sick heart hunger scarcely stung,
Nor to the beggar's language could I frame my
    tongue.

So passed another day, and so the third:
Then did I try, in vain, the crowd's resort,
In deep despair by frightful wishes stirr'd,
Near the sea-side I reached a ruined fort:
There, pains which nature could no more support,
With blindness linked, did on my vitals fall;
Dizzy my brain, with interruption short
Of hideous sense; I sunk, nor step could crawl,
And thence was borne away to neighbouring
    hospital.

Recovery came with food: but still, my brain
Was weak, nor of the past had memory.
I heard my neighbours, in their beds, complain
Of many things which never troubled me;
Of feet still bustling round with busy glee,
Of looks where common kindness had no part,
Of service done with careless cruelty,
Fretting the fever round the languid heart,
And groans, which, as they said, would make a
    dead man start.

These things just served to stir the torpid sense,
Nor pain nor pity in my bosom raised.
Memory, though slow, returned with strength;
    and thence
Dismissed, again on open day I gazed,
At houses, men, and common light, amazed.
The lanes I sought, and as the sun retired,
Came, where beneath the trees a faggot blazed;
The wild brood saw me weep, my fate enquired,
And gave me food, and rest, more welcome, more desired.

My heart is touched to think that men like these,
The rude earth's tenants, were my first relief:
How kindly did they paint their vagrant ease!
And their long holiday that feared not grief,
For all belonged to all, and each was chief.
No plough their sinews strained; on grating road
No wain they drove, and yet, the yellow sheaf
In every vale for their delight was stowed:
For them, in nature's meads, the milky udder flowed.

Semblance, with straw and panniered ass, they made
Of potters wandering on from door to door:
But life of happier sort to me pourtrayed,
And other joys my fancy to allure;
The bag-pipe dinning on the midnight moor
In barn uplighted, and companions boon
Well met from far with revelry secure,
In depth of forest glade, when jocund June
Rolled fast along the sky his warm and genial moon.

But ill it suited me, in journey dark
O'er moor and mountain, midnight theft to hatch;
To charm the surly house-dog's faithful bark,
Or hang on tiptoe at the lifted latch;

The gloomy lantern, and the dim blue match,
The black disguise, the warning whistle shrill,
And ear still busy on its nightly watch,
Were not for me, brought up in nothing ill;
Besides, on griefs so fresh my thoughts were brooding still.

What could I do, unaided and unblest?
Poor Father! gone was every friend of thine:
And kindred of dead husband are at best
Small help, and, after marriage such as mine,
With little kindness would to me incline.
Ill was I then for toil or service fit:
With tears whose course no effort could confine,
By high-way side forgetful would I sit
Whole hours, my idle arms in moping sorrow knit.

I lived upon the mercy of the fields,
And oft of cruelty the sky accused;
On hazard, or what general bounty yields,
Now coldly given, now utterly refused.
The fields I for my bed have often used:
But, what afflicts my peace with keenest ruth
Is, that I have my inner self abused,
Foregone the home delight of constant truth,
And clear and open soul, so prized in fearless youth.

Three years a wanderer, often have I view'd,
In tears, the sun towards that country tend
Where my poor heart lost all its fortitude:
And now across this moor my steps I bend –
Oh! tell me whither – for no earthly friend
Have I. – She ceased, and weeping turned away,
As if because her tale was at an end
She wept; – because she had no more to say
Of that perpetual weight which on her spirit lay.

Goody Blake and Harry Gill

A TRUE STORY

Oh! what's the matter? what's the matter?
What is't that ails young Harry Gill?
That evermore his teeth they chatter,
Chatter, chatter, chatter still.
Of waistcoats Harry has no lack,
Good duffle grey, and flannel fine;
He has a blanket on his back,
And coats enough to smother nine.

In March, December, and in July,
'Tis all the same with Harry Gill;
The neighbours tell, and tell you truly,
His teeth they chatter, chatter still.
At night, at morning, and at noon,
'Tis all the same with Harry Gill;
Beneath the sun, beneath the moon,
His teeth they chatter, chatter still.

Young Harry was a lusty drover,
And who so stout of limb as he?
His cheeks were red as ruddy clover,
His voice was like the voice of three.
Auld Goody Blake was old and poor,
Ill fed she was, and thinly clad;
And any man who pass'd her door,
Might see how poor a hut she had.

All day she spun in her poor dwelling,
And then her three hours' work at night!
Alas! 'twas hardly worth the telling,
It would not pay for candle-light.

– This woman dwelt in Dorsetshire,
Her hut was on a cold hill-side,
And in that country coals are dear,
For they come far by wind and tide.
By the same fire to boil their pottage,
Two poor old dames, as I have known,
Will often live in one small cottage,
But she, poor woman, dwelt alone.
'Twas well enough when summer came,
The long, warm, lightsome summer-day,
Then at her door the *canty* dame
Would sit, as any linnet gay.

But when the ice our streams did fetter,
Oh! then how her old bones would shake!
You would have said, if you had met her,
'Twas a hard time for Goody Blake.
Her evenings then were dull and dead;
Sad case it was, as you may think,
For very cold to go to bed,
And then for cold not sleep a wink.

Oh joy for her! when e'er in winter
The winds at night had made a rout,
And scatter'd many a lusty splinter,
And many a rotten bough about.
Yet never had she, well or sick,
As every man who knew her says,
A pile before-hand, wood or stick,
Enough to warm her for three days.

Now, when the frost was past enduring,
And made her poor old bones to ache,
Could any thing be more alluring,
Than an old hedge to Goody Blake?

And now and then, it must be said,
When her old bones were cold and chill,
She left her fire, or left her bed,
To seek the hedge of Harry Gill.

Now Harry he had long suspected
This trespass of old Goody Blake,
And vow'd that she should be detected,
And he on her would vengeance take.
And oft from his warm fire he'd go,
And to the fields his road would take,
And there, at night, in frost and snow,
He watch'd to seize old Goody Blake.

And once, behind a rick of barley,
Thus looking out did Harry stand;
The moon was full and shining clearly,
And crisp with frost the stubble-land.
– He hears a noise – he's all awake –
Again? – on tip-toe down the hill
He softly creeps – 'Tis Goody Blake,
She's at the hedge of Harry Gill.

Right glad was he when he beheld her:
Stick after stick did Goody pull,
He stood behind a bush of elder,
Till she had filled her apron full.
When with her load she turned about,
The bye-road back again to take,
He started forward with a shout,
And sprang upon poor Goody Blake.

And fiercely by the arm he took her,
And by the arm he held her fast,
And fiercely by the arm he shook her,
And cried, 'I've caught you then at last!'
Then Goody, who had nothing said,
Her bundle from her lap let fall;
And kneeling on the sticks, she pray'd
To God that is the judge of all.

She pray'd, her wither'd hand uprearing,
While Harry held her by the arm –
'God! who art never out of hearing,
'O may he never more be warm!'
The cold, cold moon above her head,
Thus on her knees did Goody pray,
Young Harry heard what she had said,
And icy-cold he turned away.

He went complaining all the morrow
That he was cold and very chill:
His face was gloom, his heart was sorrow,
Alas! that day for Harry Gill!
That day he wore a riding-coat,
But not a whit the warmer he:
Another was on Thursday brought,
And ere the Sabbath he had three.

'Twas all in vain, a useless matter,
And blankets were about him pinn'd;
Yet still his jaws and teeth they clatter,
Like a loose casement in the wind.
And Harry's flesh it fell away;
And all who see him say 'tis plain,
That, live as long as live he may,
He never will be warm again.

No word to any man he utters,
A-bed or up, to young or old;
But ever to himself he mutters,
'Poor Harry Gill is very cold.'
A-bed or up, by night or day;
His teeth they chatter, chatter still.
Now think, ye farmers all, I pray,
Of Goody Blake and Harry Gill.

Lines

WRITTEN AT A SMALL DISTANCE FROM MY HOUSE,
AND SENT BY MY LITTLE BOY TO THE PERSON
TO WHOM THEY ARE ADDRESSED

It is the first mild day of March:
Each minute sweeter than before,
The red-breast sings from the tall larch
That stands beside our door.

There is a blessing in the air,
Which seems a sense of joy to yield
To the bare trees, and mountains bare
And grass in the green field.

My Sister! ('tis a wish of mine)
Now that our morning meal is done,
Make haste, your morning task resign;
Come forth and feel the sun.

Edward will come with you, and pray,
Put on with speed your woodland dress,
And bring no book, for this one day
We'll give to idleness.

No joyless forms shall regulate
Our living Calendar:
We from to-day, my friend, will date
The opening of the year.

Love, now an universal birth,
From heart to heart is stealing,
From earth to man, from man to earth,
– It is the hour of feeling.

One moment now may give us more
Than fifty years of reason;
Our minds shall drink at every pore
The spirit of the season.

Some silent laws our hearts may make,
Which they shall long obey;
We for the year to come may take
Our temper from to-day.

And from the blessed power that rolls
About, below, above;
We'll frame the measure of our souls,
They shall be tuned to love.

Then come, my sister! come, I pray,
With speed put on your woodland dress,
And bring no book; for this one day
We'll give to idleness.

Simon Lee, the Old Huntsman
WITH AN INCIDENT IN WHICH HE WAS CONCERNED

In the sweet shire of Cardigan,
Not far from pleasant Ivor-hall,
An old man dwells, a little man,
I've heard he once was tall.
Of years he has upon his back,
No doubt, a burthen weighty;
He says he is three score and ten,
But others say he's eighty.

A long blue livery-coat has he,
That's fair behind, and fair before;
Yet, meet him where you will, you see
At once that he is poor.
Full five and twenty years he lived
A running huntsman merry;
And, though he has but one eye left,
His cheek is like a cherry.

No man like him the horn could sound,
And no man was so full of glee;
To say the least, four counties round
Had heard of Simon Lee;
His master's dead, and no one now
Dwells in the hall of Ivor;
Men, dogs, and horses, all are dead;
He is the sole survivor.

His hunting feats have him bereft
Of his right eye, as you may see:
And then, what limbs those feats have left
To poor old Simon Lee!

He has no son, he has no child,
His wife, an aged woman,
Lives with him, near the waterfall,
Upon the village common.

And he is lean and he is sick,
His little body's half awry
His ancles they are swoln and thick;
His legs are thin and dry.
When he was young he little knew
Of husbandry or tillage;
And now he's forced to work, though weak,
– The weakest in the village.

He all the country could outrun,
Could leave both man and horse behind;
And often, ere the race was done,
He reeled and was stone-blind.
And still there's something in the world
At which his heart rejoices;
For when the chiming hounds are out,
He dearly loves their voices!

Old Ruth works out of doors with him,
And does what Simon cannot do;
For she, not over stout of limb,
Is stouter of the two.
And though you with your utmost skill
From labour could not wean them,
Alas! 'tis very little, all
Which they can do between them.

Beside their moss-grown hut of clay,
Not twenty paces from the door,
A scrap of land they have, but they
Are poorest of the poor.
This scrap of land he from the heath
Enclosed when he was stronger;
But what avails the land to them,
Which they can till no longer?

Few months of life has he in store,
As he to you will tell,
For still, the more he works, the more
His poor old ancles swell.
My gentle reader, I perceive
How patiently you've waited,
And I'm afraid that you expect
Some tale will be related.

O reader! had you in your mind
Such stores as silent thought can bring,
O gentle reader! you would find
A tale in every thing.
What more I have to say is short,
I hope you'll kindly take it;
It is no tale; but should you think,
Perhaps a tale you'll make it.

One summer-day I chanced to see
This old man doing all he could
About the root of an old tree,
A stump of rotten wood.
The mattock totter'd in his hand;
So vain was his endeavour
That at the root of the old tree
He might have worked for ever.

'You're overtasked, good Simon Lee,
Give me your tool' to him I said;
And at the word right gladly he
Received my proffer'd aid.
I struck, and with a single blow
The tangled root I sever'd,
At which the poor old man so long
And vainly had endeavour'd.

The tears into his eyes were brought,
And thanks and praises seemed to run
So fast out of his heart, I thought
They never would have done.
– I've heard of hearts unkind, kind deeds
With coldness still returning.
Alas! the gratitude of men
Has oftner left me mourning.

Anecdote for Fathers,
SHEWING HOW THE ART OF LYING MAY BE TAUGHT

I have a boy of five years old,
His face is fair and fresh to see;
His limbs are cast in beauty's mould,
And dearly he loves me.

One morn we stroll'd on our dry walk,
Our quiet house all full in view,
And held such intermitted talk
As we are wont to do.

My thoughts on former pleasures ran;
I thought of Kilve's delightful shore,
My pleasant home, when spring began,
A long, long year before.

A day it was when I could bear
To think, and think, and think again;
With so much happiness to spare,
I could not feel a pain.

My boy was by my side, so slim
And graceful in his rustic dress!
And oftentimes I talked to him,
In very idleness.

The young lambs ran a pretty race;
The morning sun shone bright and warm;
'Kilve,' said I, 'was a pleasant place,
'And so is Liswyn farm.

'My little boy, which like you more,'
I said and took him by the arm –
'Our home by Kilve's delightful shore,
'Or here at Liswyn farm?'

'And tell me, had you rather be,'
I said and held him by the arm,
'At Kilve's smooth shore by the green sea,
'Or here at Liswyn farm?

In careless mood he looked at me,
While still I held him by the arm,
And said, 'At Kilve I'd rather be
'Than here at Liswyn farm.'

'Now, little Edward, say why so;
My little Edward, tell me why;'
'I cannot tell, I do not know.'
'Why this is strange,' said I.

'For, here are woods and green-hills warm;
'There surely must some reason be
'Why you would change sweet Liswyn farm
'For Kilve by the green sea.'

At this, my boy, so fair and slim,
Hung down his head, nor made reply;
And five times did I say to him,
'Why? Edward, tell me why?'

His head he raised – there was in sight,
It caught his eye, he saw it plain –
Upon the house-top, glittering bright,
A broad and gilded vane.

Then did the boy his tongue unlock,
And thus to me he made reply;
'At Kilve there was no weather-cock,
'And that's the reason why.'

O dearest, dearest boy! my heart
For better lore would seldom yearn,
Could I but teach the hundredth part
Of what from thee I learn.

We Are Seven

A simple child, dear brother Jim,
That lightly draws its breath,
And feels its life in every limb,
What should it know of death?

I met a little cottage girl,
She was eight years old, she said;
Her hair was thick with many a curl
That cluster'd round her head.

She had a rustic, woodland air,
And she was wildly clad;
Her eyes were fair, and very fair,
– Her beauty made me glad.

'Sisters and brothers, little maid,
'How many may you be?'
'How many? seven in all,' she said,
And wondering looked at me.

'And where are they, I pray you tell?'
She answered, 'Seven are we,
'And two of us at Conway dwell,
'And two are gone to sea.

'Two of us in the church-yard lie,
'My sister and my brother,
'And in the church-yard cottage, I
'Dwell near them with my mother.'

'You say that two at Conway dwell,
'And two are gone to sea,
'Yet you are seven; I pray you tell
'Sweet Maid, how this may be?'

Then did the little Maid reply,
'Seven boys and girls are we;
'Two of us in the church-yard lie,
'Beneath the church-yard tree.'

'You run about, my little maid,
'Your limbs they are alive;
'If two are in the church-yard laid,
'Then ye are only five.'

'Their graves are green, they may be seen,'
The little Maid replied,
'Twelve steps or more from my mother's door,
'And they are side by side.

'My stockings there I often knit,
'My 'kerchief there I hem;
'And there upon the ground I sit –
'I sit and sing to them.

'And often after sunset, Sir,
'When it is light and fair,
'I take my little porringer,
'And eat my supper there.

'The first that died was little Jane;
'In bed she moaning lay,
'Till God released her of her pain,
'And then she went away.

'So in the church-yard she was laid,
'And all the summer dry,
'Together round her grave we played,
'My brother John and I.

'And when the ground was white with snow,
'And I could run and slide,
'My brother John was forced to go,
'And he lies by her side,'

'How many are you then,' said I,
'If they two are in Heaven?'
The little Maiden did reply,
'O Master! we are seven.'

'But they are dead; those two are dead!
'Their spirits are in heaven!'
'Twas throwing words away; for still
The little Maid would have her will,
And said, 'Nay, we are seven!'

Lines written in Early Spring

I heard a thousand blended notes,
While in a grove I sate reclined,
In that sweet mood when pleasant thoughts
Bring sad thoughts to the mind.

To her fair works did nature link
The human soul that through me ran;
And much it griev'd my heart to think
What man has made of man.

Through primrose-tufts, in that sweet bower,
The periwinkle trail'd its wreathes;
And 'tis my faith that every flower
Enjoys the air it breathes.

The birds around me hopp'd and play'd:
Their thoughts I cannot measure,
But the least motion which they made,
It seem'd a thrill of pleasure.

The budding twigs spread out their fan,
To catch the breezy air;
And I must think, do all I can,
That there was pleasure there.

If I these thoughts may not prevent,
If such be of my creed the plan,
Have I not reason to lament
What man has made of man?

The Thorn

I

There is a thorn; it looks so old,
In truth you'd find it hard to say,
How it could ever have been young,
It looks so old and grey.
Not higher than a two-years' child,
It stands erect this aged thorn;
No leaves it has, no thorny points;
It is a mass of knotted joints,
A wretched thing forlorn.
It stands erect, and like a stone
With lichens it is overgrown.

II

Like rock or stone, it is o'ergrown
With lichens to the very top,
And hung with heavy tufts of moss,
A melancholy crop:
Up from the earth these mosses creep,
And this poor thorn they clasp it round
So close, you'd say that they were bent
With plain and manifest intent,
To drag it to the ground;
And all had joined in one endeavour
To bury this poor thorn for ever.

III

High on a mountain's highest ridge,
Where oft the stormy winter gale
Cuts like a scythe, while through the clouds
It sweeps from vale to vale;
Not five yards from the mountain-path,

This thorn you on your left espy;
And to the left, three yards beyond,
You see a little muddy pond
Of water, never dry;
I've measured it from side to side:
'Tis three feet long, and two feet wide.

IV

And close beside this aged thorn,
There is a fresh and lovely sight,
A beauteous heap, a hill of moss,
Just half a foot in height.
All lovely colours there you see,
All colours that were ever seen,
And mossy network too is there,
As if by hand of lady fair
The work had woven been,
And cups, the darlings of the eye,
So deep is their vermilion dye.

V

Ah me! what lovely tints are there!
Of olive-green and scarlet bright,
In spikes, in branches, and in stars,
Green, red, and pearly white.
This heap of earth o'ergrown with moss,
Which close beside the thorn you see,
So fresh in all its beauteous dyes,
Is like an infant's grave in size
As like as like can be:
But never, never any where,
An infant's grave was half so fair.

VI

Now would you see this aged thorn,
This pond and beauteous hill of moss,
You must take care and chuse your time
The mountain when to cross.
For oft there sits, between the heap
That's like an infant's grave in size,
And that same pond of which I spoke,
A woman in a scarlet cloak,
And to herself she cries,
'Oh misery! oh misery!
'Oh woe is me! oh misery!'

VII

At all times of the day and night
This wretched woman thither goes,
And she is known to every star,
And every wind that blows;
And there beside the thorn she sits
When the blue day-light's in the skies,
And when the whirlwind's on the hill,
Or frosty air is keen and still,
And to herself she cries,
'Oh misery! oh misery!
'Oh woe is me! oh misery!'

VIII

'Now wherefore thus, by day and night,
'In rain, in tempest, and in snow,
'Thus to the dreary mountain-top
'Does this poor woman go?
'And why sits she beside the thorn
'When the blue day-light's in the sky,
'Or when the whirlwind's on the hill,
'Or frosty air is keen and still,

'And wherefore does she cry? –
'Oh wherefore? wherefore? tell me why
'Does she repeat that doleful cry?'

IX

I cannot tell; I wish I could;
For the true reason no one knows,
But if you'd gladly view the spot,
The spot to which she goes;
The heap that's like an infant's grave,
The pond – and thorn, so old and grey,
Pass by her door – tis seldom shut –
And if you see her in her hut,
Then to the spot away! –
I never heard of such as dare
Approach the spot when she is there.

X

'But wherefore to the mountain-top
'Can this unhappy woman go,
'Whatever star is in the skies,
'Whatever wind may blow?'
Nay rack your brain – 'tis all in vain,
I'll tell you every thing I know;
But to the thorn, and to the pond
Which is a little step beyond,
I wish that you would go:
Perhaps when you are at the place
You something of her tale may trace.

XI

I'll give you the best help I can:
Before you up the mountain go,
Up to the dreary mountain-top,
I'll tell you all I know.

'Tis now some two and twenty years,
Since she (her name is Martha Ray)
Gave with a maiden's true good will
Her company to Stephen Hill;
And she was blithe and gay,
And she was happy, happy still
Whene'er she thought of Stephen Hill.

XII

And they had fix'd the wedding-day,
The morning that must wed them both;
But Stephen to another maid
Had sworn another oath;
And with this other maid to church
Unthinking Stephen went –
Poor Martha! on that woful day
A cruel, cruel fire, they say,
Into her bones was sent:
It dried her body like a cinder,
And almost turn'd her brain to tinder.

XIII

They say, full six months after this,
While yet the summer-leaves were green,
She to the mountain-top would go,
And there was often seen.
'Tis said, a child was in her womb,
As now to any eye was plain;
She was with child, and she was mad,
Yet often she was sober sad
From her exceeding pain.
Oh me! ten thousand times I'd rather
That he had died, that cruel father!

XIV

Sad case for such a brain to hold
Communion with a stirring child!
Sad case, as you may think, for one
Who had a brain so wild!
Last Christmas when we talked of this,
Old Farmer Simpson did maintain,
That in her womb the infant wrought
About its mother's heart, and brought
Her senses back again:
And when at last her time drew near,
Her looks were calm, her senses clear.

XV

No more I know, I wish I did,
And I would tell it all to you;
For what became of this poor child
There's none that ever knew:
And if a child was born or no,
There's no one that could ever tell;
And if 'twas born alive or dead,
There's no one knows, as I have said,
But some remember well,
That Martha Ray about this time
Would up the mountain often climb.

XVI

And all that winter, when at night
The wind blew from the mountain-peak,
'Twas worth your while, though in the dark,
The church-yard path to seek:
For many a time and oft were heard
Cries coming from the mountain-head,
Some plainly living voices were,

And others, I've heard many swear,
Were voices of the dead:
I cannot think, whate'er they say,
They had to do with Martha Ray.

XVII

But that she goes to this old thorn,
The thorn which I've described to you,
And there sits in a scarlet cloak,
I will be sworn is true.
For one day with my telescope,
To view the ocean wide and bright,
When to this country first I came,
Ere I had heard of Martha's name,
I climbed the mountain's height:
A storm came on, and I could see
No object higher than my knee.

XVIII

'Twas mist and rain, and storm and rain,
No screen, no fence could I discover,
And then the wind! in faith, it was
A wind full ten times over.
I looked around, I thought I saw
A jutting crag, and off I ran,
Head-foremost, through the driving rain,
The shelter of the crag to gain,
And, as I am a man,
Instead of jutting crag, I found
A woman seated on the ground.

XIX

I did not speak – I saw her face,
Her face it was enough for me;
I turned about and heard her cry,

'O misery! O misery!'
And there she sits, until the moon
Through half the clear blue sky will go,
And when the little breezes make
The waters of the pond to shake,
As all the country know,
She shudders and you hear her cry,
'Oh misery! oh misery!

XX

'But what's the thorn? and what's the pond?
'And what's the hill of moss to her?
'And what's the creeping breeze that comes
'The little pond to stir?'
I cannot tell; but some will say
She hanged her baby on the tree,
Some say she drowned it in the pond,
Which is a little step beyond,
But all and each agree,
The little babe was buried there,
Beneath that hill of moss so fair.

XXI

I've heard the scarlet moss is red
With drops of that poor infant's blood;
But kill a new-born infant thus!
I do not think she could.
Some say, if to the pond you go,
And fix on it a steady view,
The shadow of a babe you trace,
A baby and a baby's face,
And that it looks at you;
Whene'er you look on it, 'tis plain
The baby looks at you again.

XXII

And some had sworn an oath that she
Should be to public justice brought;
And for the little infant's bones
With spades they would have sought.
But then the beauteous hill of moss
Before their eyes began to stir;
And for full fifty yards around,
The grass it shook upon the ground;
But all do still aver
The little babe is buried there,
Beneath that hill of moss so fair.

XXIII

I cannot tell how this may be,
But plain it is, the thorn is bound
With heavy tufts of moss, that strive
To drag it to the ground.
And this I know, full many a time,
When she was on the mountain high,
By day, and in the silent night,
When all the stars shone clear and bright,
That I have heard her cry,
'Oh misery! oh misery!
'O woe is me! oh misery!'

The Last of the Flock

In distant countries I have been,
And yet I have not often seen
A healthy man, a man full grown,
Weep in the public roads alone.
But such a one, on English ground,
And in the broad high-way, I met;
Along the broad high-way he came,
His cheeks with tears were wet.
Sturdy he seemed, though he was sad;
And in his arms a lamb he had.

He saw me, and he turned aside,
As if he wished himself to hide:
Then with his coat he made essay
To wipe those briny tears away.
I follow'd him, and said, 'My friend
'What ails you? wherefore weep you so?'
– 'Shame on me, Sir! this lusty lamb,
He makes my tears to flow.
To-day I fetched him from the rock;
He is the last of all my flock.

When I was young, a single man,
And after youthful follies ran,
Though little given to care and thought,
Yet, so it was, a ewe I bought;
And other sheep from her I raised,
As healthy sheep as you might see,
And then I married, and was rich
As I could wish to be;
Of sheep I number'd a full score,
And every year encreas'd my store.

Year after year my stock it grew,
And from this one, this single ewe,
Full fifty comely sheep I raised,
As sweet a flock as ever grazed!
Upon the mountain did they feed;
They throve, and we at home did thrive.
– This lusty lamb of all my store
Is all that is alive:
And now I care not if we die,
And perish all of poverty.

Ten children, Sir! had I to feed,
Hard labour in a time of need!
My pride was tamed, and in our grief
I of the parish ask'd relief.
They said I was a wealthy man;
My sheep upon the mountain fed,
And it was fit that thence I took
Whereof to buy us bread:'
'Do this; how can we give to you,'
They cried, 'what to the poor is due?'

I sold a sheep as they had said,
And bought my little children bread,
And they were healthy with their food;
For me it never did me good.
A woeful time it was for me,
To see the end of all my gains,
The pretty flock which I had reared
With all my care and pains,
To see it melt like snow away!
For me it was a woeful day.

Another still! and still another!
A little lamb, and then its mother!
It was a vein that never stopp'd,
Like blood-drops from my heart they dropp'd.
Till thirty were not left alive
They dwindled, dwindled, one by one,
And I may say that many a time
I wished they all were gone:
They dwindled one by one away;
For me it was a woeful day.

To wicked deeds I was inclined,
And wicked fancies cross'd my mind,
And every man I chanc'd to see,
I thought he knew some ill of me.
No peace, no comfort could I find,
No ease, within doors or without,
And crazily, and wearily,
I went my work about.
Oft-times I thought to run away;
For me it was a woeful day.

Sir! 'twas a precious flock to me,
As dear as my own children be;
For daily with my growing store
I loved my children more and more.
Alas! it was an evil time;
God cursed me in my sore distress,
I prayed, yet every day I thought
I loved my children less;
And every week, and every day,
My flock, it seemed to melt away.

They dwindled, Sir, sad sight to see!
From ten to five, from five to three,
A lamb, a weather, and a ewe;
And then at last, from three to two;
And of my fifty, yesterday
I had but only one,
And here it lies upon my arm,
Alas! and I have none;
To-day I fetched it from the rock;
It is the last of all my flock.'

The Dungeon

And this place our forefathers made for man!
This is the process of our love and wisdom,
To each poor brother who offends against us –
Most innocent, perhaps – and what if guilty?
Is this the only cure? Merciful God!
Each pore and natural outlet shrivell'd up
By ignorance and parching poverty,
His energies roll back upon his heart,
And stagnate and corrupt; till changed to poison,
They break out on him, like a loathsome plague-spot;
Then we call in our pamper'd mountebanks –
And this is their best cure! uncomforted
And friendless solitude, groaning and tears,
And savage faces, at the clanking hour,
Seen through the steams and vapour of his dungeon,
By the lamp's dismal twilight! So he lies
Circled with evil, till his very soul
Unmoulds its essence, hopelessly deformed
By sights of ever more deformity!

With other ministrations thou, O nature!
Healest thy wandering and distempered child:
Thou pourest on him thy soft influences,
Thy sunny hues, fair forms, and breathing sweets,
Thy melodies of woods, and winds, and waters,
Till he relent, and can no more endure
To be a jarring and a dissonant thing,
Amid this general dance and minstrelsy;
But, bursting into tears, wins back his way,
His angry spirit healed and harmonized
By the benignant touch of love and beauty.

The Mad Mother

Her eyes are wild, her head is bare,
The sun has burnt her coal-black hair,
Her eye-brows have a rusty stain,
And she came far from over the main.
She has a baby on her arm,
Or else she were alone;
And underneath the hay-stack warm,
And on the green-wood stone,
She talked and sung the woods among;
And it was in the English tongue.

'Sweet babe! they say that I am mad,
But nay, my heart is far too glad;
And I am happy when I sing
Full many a sad and doleful thing:
Then, lovely baby, do not fear!
I pray thee have no fear of me,
But, safe as in a cradle, here
My lovely baby! thou shalt be,
To thee I know too much I owe;
I cannot work thee any woe.

A fire was once within my brain;
And in my head a dull, dull pain;
And fiendish faces one, two, three,
Hung at my breasts, and pulled at me.
But then there came a sight of joy;
It came at once to do me good;
I waked, and saw my little boy,
My little boy of flesh and blood;
Oh joy for me that sight to see!
For he was here, and only he.

Suck, little babe, oh suck again!
It cools my blood; it cools my brain;
Thy lips I feel them, baby! they
Draw from my heart the pain away.
Oh! press me with thy little hand;
It loosens something at my chest;
About that tight and deadly band
I feel thy little fingers press'd.
The breeze I see is in the tree;
It comes to cool my babe and me.

Oh! love me, love me, little boy!
Thou art thy mother's only joy;
And do not dread the waves below,
When o'er the sea-rock's edge we go;
The high crag cannot work me harm,
Nor leaping torrents when they howl;
The babe I carry on my arm,
He saves for me my precious soul;
Then happy lie, for blest am I;
Without me my sweet babe would die.

Then do not fear, my boy! for thee
Bold as a lion I will be;
And I will always be thy guide,
Through hollow snows and rivers wide.
I'll build an Indian bower; I know
The leaves that make the softest bed:
And if from me thou wilt not go,
But still be true 'till I am dead,
My pretty thing! then thou shalt sing,
As merry as the birds in spring.

Thy father cares not for my breast,
'Tis thine, sweet baby, there to rest:
'Tis all thine own! and if its hue
Be changed, that was so fair to view,
'Tis fair enough for thee, my dove!
My beauty, little child, is flown;
But thou wilt live with me in love,
And what if my poor cheek be brown?
'Tis well for me; thou canst not see
How pale and wan it else would be.

Dread not their taunts, my little life!
I am thy father's wedded wife;
And underneath the spreading tree
We two will live in honesty.
If his sweet boy he could forsake,
With me he never would have stay'd:
From him no harm my babe can take,
But he, poor man! is wretched made,
And every day we two will pray
For him that's gone and far away.

I'll teach my boy the sweetest things;
I'll teach him how the owlet sings.
My little babe! thy lips are still,
And thou has almost suck'd thy fill.
– Where art thou gone my own dear child?
What wicked looks are those I see?
Alas! alas! that look so wild,
It never, never came from me:
If thou art mad, my pretty lad,
Then I must be for ever sad.

Oh! smile on me, my little lamb!
For I thy own dear mother am.
My love for thee has well been tried:
I've sought thy father far and wide.
I know the poisons of the shade,
I know the earth-nuts fit for food;
Then, pretty dear, be not afraid;
We'll find thy father in the wood.
Now laugh and be gay, to the woods away!
And there, my babe; we'll live for aye.

The Idiot Boy

'Tis eight o'clock, – a clear March night,
The moon is up – the sky is blue,
The owlet in the moonlight air,
He shouts from nobody knows where;
He lengthens out his lonely shout,
Halloo! halloo! a long halloo!

– Why bustle thus about your door,
What means this bustle, Betty Foy?
Why are you in this mighty fret?
And why on horseback have you set
Him whom you love, your idiot boy?

Beneath the moon that shines so bright,
Till she is tired, let Betty Foy
With girt and stirrup fiddle-faddle;
But wherefore set upon a saddle
Him whom she loves, her idiot boy?

There's scarce a soul that's out of bed;
Good Betty! put him down again;
His lips with joy they burr at you,
But, Betty! what has he to do
With stirrup, saddle, or with rein?

The world will say 'tis very idle,
Bethink you of the time of night;
There's not a mother, no not one,
But when she hears what you have done,
Oh! Betty she'll be in a fright.

But Betty's bent on her intent,
For her good neighbour, Susan Gale,
Old Susan, she who dwells alone,
Is sick, and makes a piteous moan,
As if her very life would fail.

There's not a house within a mile,
No hand to help them in distress:
Old Susan lies a bed in pain,
And sorely puzzled are the twain,
For what she ails they cannot guess.

And Betty's husband's at the wood,
Where by the week he doth abide,
A woodman in the distant vale;
There's none to help poor Susan Gale,
What must be done? what will betide?

And Betty from the lane has fetched
Her pony, that is mild and good,
Whether he be in joy or pain,
Feeding at will along the lane,
Or bringing faggots from the wood.

And he is all in travelling trim,
And by the moonlight, Betty Foy
Has up upon the saddle set,
The like was never heard of yet,
Him whom she loves, her idiot boy.

And he must post without delay
Across the bridge that's in the dale,
And by the church, and o'er the down,
To bring a doctor from the town,
Or she will die, old Susan Gale.

There is no need of boot or spur,
There is no need of whip or wand,
For Johnny has his holly-bough,
And with a hurly-burly now
He shakes the green bough in his hand.

And Betty o'er and o'er has told
The boy who is her best delight,
Both what to follow, what to shun,
What do, and what to leave undone,
How turn to left, and how to right.

And Betty's most especial charge,
Was, 'Johnny! Johnny! mind that you
'Come home again, nor stop at all,
'Come home again, whate'er befal,
'My Johnny do, I pray you do.'

To this did Johnny answer make,
Both with his head, and with his hand,
And proudly shook the bridle too,
And then! his words were not a few,
Which Betty well could understand.

And now that Johnny is just going,
Though Betty's in a mighty flurry,
She gently pats the pony's side,
On which her idiot boy must ride,
And seems no longer in a hurry.

But when the pony moved his legs,
Oh! then for the poor idiot boy!
For joy he cannot hold the bridle,
For joy his head and heels are idle,
He's idle all for very joy.

And while the pony moves his legs,
In Johnny's left-hand you may see,
The green bough's motionless and dead;
The moon that shines above his head
Is not more still and mute than he.

His heart it was so full of glee,
That till full fifty yards were gone,
He quite forgot his holly whip,
And all his skill in horsemanship,
Oh! happy, happy, happy John.

And Betty's standing at the door,
And Betty's face with joy o'erflows,
Proud of herself, and proud of him,
She sees him in his travelling trim;
How quietly her Johnny goes.

The silence of her idiot boy,
What hopes it sends to Betty's heart!
He's at the guide-post – he turns right,
She watches till he's out of sight,
And Betty will not then depart.

Burr, burr – now Johnny's lips they burr,
As loud as any mill, or near it,
Meek as a lamb the pony moves,
And Johnny makes the noise he loves,
And Betty listens, glad to hear it.

Away she hies to Susan Gale:
And Johnny's in a merry tune,
The owlets hoot, the owlets curr,
And Johnny's lips they burr, burr, burr,
And on he goes beneath the moon.

His steed and he right well agree,
For of this pony there's a rumour,
That should he lose his eyes and ears,
And should he live a thousand years,
He never will be out of humour.

But then he is a horse that thinks!
And when he thinks his pace is slack;
Now, though he knows poor Johnny well,
Yet for his life he cannot tell
What he has got upon his back.

So through the moonlight lanes they go,
And far into the moonlight dale,
And by the church, and o'er the down,
To bring a doctor from the town,
To comfort poor old Susan Gale.

And Betty, now at Susan's side,
Is in the middle of her story,
What comfort Johnny soon will bring,
With many a most diverting thing,
Of Johnny's wit and Johnny's glory.

And Betty's still at Susan's side:
By this time she's not quite so flurried;
Demure with porringer and plate
She sits, as if in Susan's fate
Her life and soul were buried.

But Betty, poor good woman! she,
You plainly in her face may read it,
Could lend out of that moment's store
Five years of happiness or more,
To any that might need it.

But yet I guess that now and then
With Betty all was not so well,
And to the road she turns her ears,
And thence full many a sound she hears,
Which she to Susan will not tell.

Poor Susan moans, poor Susan groans,
'As sure as there's a moon in heaven,'
Cries Betty, 'he'll be back again;
'They'll both be here, 'tis almost ten,
'They'll both be here before eleven.'

Poor Susan moans, poor Susan groans,
The clock gives warning for eleven;
'Tis on the stroke – 'If Johnny's near,'
Quoth Betty 'he will soon be here,
'As sure as there's a moon in heaven.'

The clock is on the stroke of twelve,
And Johnny is not yet in sight,
The moon's in heaven, as Betty sees,
But Betty is not quite at ease;
And Susan has a dreadful night.

And Betty, half an hour ago,
On Johnny vile reflections cast;
'A little idle sauntering thing!'
With other names, an endless string,
But now that time is gone and past.

And Betty's drooping at the heart,
That happy time all past and gone,
'How can it be he is so late?
'The doctor he has made him wait,
'Susan! they'll both be here anon.'

And Susan's growing worse and worse,
And Betty's in a sad quandary;
And then there's nobody to say
If she must go or she must stay:
– She's in a sad quandary.

The clock is on the stroke of one;
But neither Doctor nor his guide
Appear along the moonlight road,
There's neither horse nor man abroad,
And Betty's still at Susan's side.

And Susan she begins to fear
Of sad mischances not a few,
That Johnny may perhaps be drown'd,
Or lost perhaps, and never found;
Which they must both for ever rue.

She prefaced half a hint of this
With, 'God forbid it should be true!'
At the first word that Susan said
Cried Betty, rising from the bed,
'Susan, I'd gladly stay with you.

'I must be gone, I must away,
'Consider, Johnny's but half-wise;
'Susan, we must take care of him,
'If he is hurt in life or limb' –
'Oh God forbid!' poor Susan cries.

'What can I do?' says Betty, going,
'What can I do to ease your pain?
'Good Susan tell me, and I'll stay;
'I fear you're in a dreadful way,
'But I shall soon be back again.'

'Good Betty go, good Betty go,
'There's nothing that can ease my pain.'
Then off she hies, but with a prayer
That God poor Susan's life would spare,
Till she comes back again.

So, through the moonlight lane she goes,
And far into the moonlight dale;
And how she ran, and how she walked,
And all that to herself she talked,
Would surely be a tedious tale.

In high and low, above, below,
In great and small, in round and square,
In tree and tower was Johnny seen,
In bush and brake, in black and green,
'Twas Johnny, Johnny, every where.

She's past the bridge that's in the dale,
And now the thought torments her sore,
Johnny perhaps his horse forsook,
To hunt the moon that's in the brook,
And never will be heard of more.

And now she's high upon the down,
Alone amid a prospect wide;
There's neither Johnny nor his horse,
Among the fern or in the gorse;
There's neither doctor nor his guide.

'Oh saints! what is become of him?
'Perhaps he's climbed into an oak,
'Where he will stay till he is dead;
'Or sadly he has been misled,
'And joined the wandering gypsey-folk.

'Or him that wicked pony's carried
'To the dark cave, the goblins' hall,
'Or in the castle he's pursuing,
'Among the ghosts, his own undoing;
'Or playing with the waterfall.'

At poor old Susan then she railed,
While to the town she posts away;
'If Susan had not been so ill,
'Alas! I should have had him still,
'My Johnny, till my dying day.'

Poor Betty! in this sad distemper,
The doctor's self would hardly spare,
Unworthy things she talked and wild,
Even he, of cattle the most mild,
The pony had his share.

And now she's got into the town,
And to the doctor's door she hies;
'Tis silence all on every side;
The town so long, the town so wide,
Is silent as the skies.

And now she's at the doctor's door,
She lifts the knocker, rap, rap, rap,
The doctor at the casement shews,
His glimmering eyes that peep and doze;
And one hand rubs his old night-cap.

'Oh Doctor! Doctor! where's my Johnny?'
'I'm here, what is't you want with me?'
'Oh Sir! you know I'm Betty Foy,
'And I have lost my poor dear boy,
'You know him – him you often see;

'He's not so wise as some folks be,'
'The devil take his wisdom!' said
The Doctor, looking somewhat grim,
'What, woman! should I know of him?'
And, grumbling, he went back to bed.

'O woe is me! O woe is me!
'Here will I die; here will I die;
'I thought to find my Johnny here,
'But he is neither far nor near,
'Oh! what a wretched mother I!'

She stops, she stands, she looks about,
Which way to turn she cannot tell.
Poor Betty! it would ease her pain
If she had heart to knock again;
– The clock strikes three – a dismal knell!

Then up along the town she hies,
No wonder if her senses fail,
This piteous news so much it shock'd her,
She quite forgot to send the Doctor,
To comfort poor old Susan Gale.

And now she's high upon the down,
And she can see a mile of road,
'Oh cruel! I'm almost three-score;
'Such night as this was ne'er before,
'There's not a single soul abroad.'

She listens, but she cannot hear
The foot of horse, the voice of man;
The streams with softest sound are flowing,
The grass you almost hear it growing,
You hear it now if e'er you can.

The owlets through the long blue night
Are shouting to each other still:
Fond lovers, yet not quite hob nob,
They lengthen out the tremulous sob,
That echoes far from hill to hill.

Poor Betty now has lost all hope,
Her thoughts are bent on deadly sin;
A green-grown pond she just has pass'd,
And from the brink she hurries fast,
Lest she should drown herself therein.

And now she sits her down and weeps;
Such tears she never shed before;
'Oh dear, dear pony! my sweet joy!
'Oh carry back my idiot boy!
'And we will ne'er o'erload thee more.'

A thought is come into her head;
'The pony he is mild and good,
'And we have always used him well;
'Perhaps he's gone along the dell,
'And carried Johnny to the wood.'

Then up she springs as if on wings;
She thinks no more of deadly sin;
If Betty fifty ponds should see,
The last of all her thoughts would be,
To drown herself therein.

Oh reader! now that I might tell
What Johnny and his horse are doing!
What they've been doing all this time,
Oh could I put it into rhyme,
A most delightful tale pursuing!

Perhaps, and no unlikely thought!
He with his pony now doth roam
The cliffs and peaks so high that are,
To lay his hands upon a star,
And in his pocket bring it home.

Perhaps he's turned himself about,
His face unto his horse's tail,
And still and mute, in wonder lost,
All like a silent horseman-ghost,
He travels on along the vale.

And now, perhaps, he's hunting sheep,
A fierce and dreadful hunter he!
Yon valley, that's so trim and green,
In five months' time, should he be seen,
A desart wilderness will be.

Perhaps, with head and heels on fire,
And like the very soul of evil,
He's galloping away, away,
And so he'll gallop on for aye,
The bane of all that dread the devil.

I to the muses have been bound,
These fourteen years, by strong indentures;
Oh gentle muses! let me tell
But half of what to him befel,
Fore sure he met with strange adventures.

Oh gentle muses! is this kind?
Why will ye thus my suit repel?
Why of your further aid bereave me?
And can ye thus unfriended leave me?
Ye muses! whom I love so well.

Who's yon, that, near the waterfall,
Which thunders down with headlong force,
Beneath the moon, yet shining fair,
As careless as if nothing were,
Sits upright on a feeding horse?

Unto his horse, that's feeding free,
He seems, I think, the rein to give;
Of moon or stars he takes no heed;
Of such we in romances read,
– 'Tis Johnny! Johnny! as I live.

And that's the very pony too.
Where is she, where is Betty Foy?
She hardly can sustain her fears;
The roaring water-fall she hears,
And cannot find her idiot boy.

Your pony's worth his weight in gold,
Then calm your terrors, Betty Foy!
She's coming from among the trees,
And now, all full in view, she sees
Him whom she loves, her idiot boy.

And Betty sees the pony too:
Why stand you thus Good Betty Foy?
It is no goblin, 'tis no ghost,
'Tis he whom you so long have lost,
He whom you love, your idiot boy.

She looks again – her arms are up –
She screams – she cannot move for joy;
She darts as with a torrent's force,
She almost has o'erturned the horse,
And fast she holds her idiot boy.

And Johnny burrs and laughs aloud,
Whether in cunning or in joy,
I cannot tell; but while he laughs,
Betty a drunken pleasure quaffs,
To hear again her idiot boy.

And now she's at the pony's tail,
And now she's at the pony's head,
On that side now, and now on this,
And almost stifled with her bliss,
A few sad tears does Betty shed.

She kisses o'er and o'er again,
Him whom she loves, her idiot boy,
She's happy here, she's happy there,
She is uneasy every where;
Her limbs are all alive with joy.

She pats the pony, where or when
She knows not, happy Betty Foy!
The little pony glad may be,
But he is milder far than she,
You hardly can perceive his joy.

'Oh! Johnny, never mind the Doctor;
'You've done your best, and that is all.'
She took the reins, when this was said,
And gently turned the pony's head
From the loud water-fall.

By this the stars were almost gone,
The moon was setting on the hill,
So pale you scarcely looked at her:
The little birds began to stir,
Though yet their tongues were still.

The pony, Betty, and her boy,
Wind slowly through the woody dale:
And who is she, be-times abroad,
That hobbles up the steep rough road?
Who is it, but old Susan Gale?

Long Susan lay deep lost in thought,
And many dreadful fears beset her,
Both for her messenger and nurse;
And as her mind grew worse and worse,
Her body it grew better.

She turned, she toss'd herself in bed,
On all sides doubts and terrors met her;
Point after point did she discuss;
And while her mind was fighting thus,
Her body still grew better.

'Alas! what is become of them?
'These fears can never be endured,
'I'll to the wood.' – The word scarce said,
Did Susan rise up from her bed,
As if by magic cured.

Away she posts up hill and down,
And to the wood at length is come,
She spies her friends, she shouts a greeting;
Oh me! it is a merry meeting,
As ever was in Christendom.

The owls have hardly sung their last,
While our four travellers homeward wend;
The owls have hooted all night long,
And with the owls began my song,
And with the owls must end.

For while they all were travelling home,
Cried Betty, 'Tell us Johnny, do,
'Where all this long night you have been,
'What you have heard, what you have seen,
'And Johnny, mind you tell us true.'

Now Johnny all night long had heard
The owls in tuneful concert strive;
No doubt too he the moon had seen;
For in the moonlight he had been
From eight o'clock till five.

And thus to Betty's question, he
Made answer, like a traveller bold,
(His very words I give to you,)
'The cocks did crow to-whoo, to-whoo,
'And the sun did shine so cold.'
– Thus answered Johnny in his glory,
And that was all his travel's story.

Lines written near Richmond,
upon the Thames, at Evening

How rich the wave, in front, imprest
With evening-twilight's summer hues,
While, facing thus the crimson west,
The boat her silent path pursues!
And see how dark the backward stream!
A little moment past, so smiling!
And still, perhaps, with faithless gleam,
Some other loiterer beguiling.

Such views the youthful bard allure,
But, heedless of the following gloom,
He deems their colours shall endure
'Till peace go with him to the tomb.
– And let him nurse his fond deceit,
And what if he must die in sorrow!
Who would not cherish dreams so sweet,
Though grief and pain may come to-morrow?

Glide gently, thus for ever glide,
O Thames! that other bards may see,
As lovely visions by thy side
As now, fair river! come to me.
Oh glide, fair stream! for ever so;
Thy quiet soul on all bestowing,
'Till all our minds for ever flow,
As thy deep waters now are flowing.

Vain thought! yet be as now thou art,
That in thy waters may be seen
The image of a poet's heart,
How bright, how solemn, how serene!

Such heart did once the poet bless,
Who, pouring here a* *later* ditty,
Could find no refuge from distress,
But in the milder grief of pity.

Remembrance! as we glide along,
For him suspend the dashing oar,
And pray that never child of Song
May know his freezing sorrows more.
How calm! how still! the only sound,
The dripping of the oar suspended!
– The evening darkness gathers round
By virtue's holiest powers attended.

* Collins's Ode on the death of Thomson, the last written, I believe, of the
poems which were published during his lifetime. This Ode is also alluded to
in the next stanza.

Expostulation and Reply

'Why William, on that old grey stone,
'Thus for the length of half a day,
'Why William, sit you thus alone,
'And dream your time away?

'Where are your books? that light bequeath'd
'To beings else forlorn and blind!
'Up! Up! and drink the spirit breath'd
'From dead men to their kind.

'You look round on your mother earth,
'As if she for no purpose bore you;
'As if you were her first-born birth,
'And none had lived before you!'

One morning thus, by Esthwaite lake,
When life was sweet I knew not why,
To me my good friend Matthew spake,
And thus I made reply.

'The eye it cannot chuse but see,
'We cannot bid the ear be still;
'Our bodies feel, where'er they be,
'Against, or with our will

'Nor less I deem that there are powers,
'Which of themselves our minds impress,
'That we can feed this mind of ours,
'In a wise passiveness.

'Think you, mid all this mighty sum
'Of things for ever speaking,
'That nothing of itself will come,
'But we must still be seeking?

'– Then ask not wherefore, here, alone,
'Conversing as I may,
'I sit upon this old grey stone,
'And dream my time away.'

The Tables Turned
AN EVENING SCENE, ON THE SAME SUBJECT

Up! up! my friend, and clear your looks,
Why all this toil and trouble?
Up! up! my friend, and quit your books,
Or surely you'll grow double.

The sun above the mountain's head,
A freshening lustre mellow,
Through all the long green fields has spread,
His first sweet evening yellow.

Books! 'tis a dull and endless strife,
Come, hear the woodland linnet,
How sweet his music; on my life
There's more of wisdom in it.

And hark! how blithe the throstle sings!
And he is no mean preacher;
Come forth into the light of things,
Let Nature be your teacher.

She has a world of ready wealth,
Our minds and hearts to bless –
Spontaneous wisdom breathed by health,
Truth breathed by chearfulness.

One impulse from a vernal wood
May teach you more of man;
Of moral evil and of good,
Than all the sages can.

Sweet is the lore which nature brings;
Our meddling intellect
Mis-shapes the beauteous forms of things;
– We murder to dissect.

Enough of science and of art;
Close up these barren leaves;
Come forth, and bring with you a heart
That watches and receives.

Old Man Travelling
ANIMAL TRANQUILLITY AND DECAY, A SKETCH

> The little hedge-row birds,
That peck along the road, regard him not.
He travels on, and in his face, his step,
His gait, is one expression; every limb,
His look and bending figure, all bespeak
A man who does not move with pain, but moves
With thought – He is insensibly subdued
To settled quiet: he is one by whom
All effort seems forgotten, one to whom
Long patience has such mild composure given,
That patience now doth seem a thing, of which
He hath no need. He is by nature led
To peace so perfect, that the young behold
With envy, what the old man hardly feels.
– I asked him whither he was bound, and what
The object of his journey; he replied
'Sir! I am going many miles to take
'A last leave of my son, a mariner,
'Who from a sea-fight has been brought to
        Falmouth,
And there is dying in an hospital.'

The Complaint of a Forsaken Indian Woman

[*When a Northern Indian, from sickness, is unable to continue his journey with his companions; he is left behind, covered over with Deer-skins, and is supplied with water, food, and fuel if the situation of the place will afford it. He is informed of the track which his companions intend to pursue, and if he is unable to follow, or overtake them, he perishes alone in the Desart; unless he should have the good fortune to fall in with some other Tribes of Indians. It is unnecessary to add that the females are equally, or still more, exposed to the same fate. See that very interesting work,* Hearne's Journey *from* Hudson's Bay *to the* Northern Ocean. *When the Northern Lights, as the same writer informs us, vary their position in the air, they make a rustling and a crackling noise. This circumstance is alluded to in the first stanza of the following poem.*]

The Complaint, &c.

Before I see another day,
Oh let my body die away!
In sleep I heard the northern gleams;
The stars they were among my dreams;
In sleep did I behold the skies,
I saw the crackling flashes drive;
And yet they are upon my eyes,
And yet I am alive.
Before I see another day,
Oh let my body die away!

My fire is dead: it knew no pain;
Yet is it dead, and I remain.
All stiff with ice the ashes lie;
And they are dead, and I will die.
When I was well, I wished to live,

For clothes, for warmth, for food, and fire;
But they to me no joy can give,
No pleasure now, and no desire.
Then here contented will I lie;
Alone I cannot fear to die.

Alas! you might have dragged me on
Another day, a single one!
Too soon despair o'er me prevailed;
Too soon my heartless spirit failed;
When you were gone my limbs were stronger,
And Oh how grievously I rue,
That, afterwards, a little longer,
My friends, I did not follow you!
For strong and without pain I lay,
My friends, when you were gone away.

My child! they gave thee to another,
A woman who was not thy mother.
When from my arms my babe they took,
On me how strangely did he look!
Through his whole body something ran,
A most strange something did I see;
– As if he strove to be a man,
That he might pull the sledge for me.
And then he stretched his arms, how wild!
Oh mercy! like a little child.

My little joy! my little pride!
In two days more I must have died.
Then do not weep and grieve for me;
I feel I must have died with thee.
Oh wind that o'er my head art flying,
The way my friends their course did bend,
I should not feel the pain of dying,

Could I with thee a message send.
Too soon, my friends, you went away;
For I had many things to say.

I'll follow you across the snow,
You travel heavily and slow:
In spite of all my weary pain,
I'll look upon your tents again.
My fire is dead, and snowy white
The water which beside it stood;
The wolf has come to me to-night,
And he has stolen away my food.
For ever left alone am I,
Then wherefore should I fear to die?

My journey will be shortly run,
I shall not see another sun,
I cannot lift my limbs to know
If they have any life or no.
My poor forsaken child! if I
For once could have thee close to me,
With happy heart I then would die,
And my last thoughts would happy be.
I feel my body die away,
I shall not see another day.

The Convict

The glory of evening was spread through the west;
   – On the slope of a mountain I stood,
While the joy that precedes the calm season of rest
   Rang loud through the meadow and wood.

'And must we then part from a dwelling so fair?'
   In the pain of my spirit I said,
And with a deep sadness I turned, to repair
   To the cell where the convict is laid.

The thick-ribbed walls that o'ershadow the gate
   Resound; and the dungeons unfold:
I pause; and at length, through the glimmering grate,
   That outcast of pity behold.

His black matted head on his shoulder is bent,
   And deep is the sigh of his breath,
And with stedfast dejection his eyes are intent
   On the fetters that link him to death.

'Tis sorrow enough on that visage to gaze,
   That body dismiss'd from his care;
Yet my fancy has pierced to his heart, and pourtrays
   More terrible images there.

His bones are consumed, and his life-blood is dried,
   With wishes the past to undo;
And his crime, through the pains that o'erwhelm him,
     descried,
   Still blackens and grows on his view.

When from the dark synod, or blood-reeking field,
    To his chamber the monarch is led,
All soothers of sense their soft virtue shall yield,
    And quietness pillow his head.

But if grief, self-consumed, in oblivion would doze,
    And conscience her tortures appease,
'Mid tumult and uproar this man must repose;
    In the comfortless vault of disease.

When his fetters at night have so press'd on his limbs,
    That the weight can no longer be borne,
If, while a half-slumber his memory bedims,
    The wretch on his pallet should turn,

While the jail-mastiff howls at the dull clanking chain,
    From the roots of his hair there shall start
A thousand sharp punctures of cold-sweating pain,
    And terror shall leap at his heart.

But now he half-raises his deep-sunken eye,
    And the motion unsettles a tear;
The silence of sorrow it seems to supply,
    And asks of me why I am here.

'Poor victim! no idle intruder has stood
    'With o'erweening complacence our state to compare,
'But one, whose first wish is the wish to be good,
    'Is come as a brother thy sorrows to share.

'At thy name though compassion her nature resign,
    'Though in virtue's proud mouth thy report be a stain,
'My care, if the arm of the mighty were mine,
    'Would plant thee where yet thou might'st blossom
      again.'

Lines written a few miles above *Tintern Abbey*
ON REVISITING THE BANKS OF THE WYE
DURING A TOUR, JULY 13, 1798

Five years have passed; five summers, with the length
Of five long winters! and again I hear
These waters, rolling from their mountain-springs
With a sweet inland murmur.* – Once again
Do I behold these steep and lofty cliffs,
Which on a wild secluded scene impress
Thoughts of more deep seclusion; and connect
The landscape with the quiet of the sky.
The day is come when I again repose
Here, under this dark sycamore, and view
These plots of cottage-ground, these orchard-tufts,
Which, at this season, with their unripe fruits,
Among the woods and copses lose themselves,
Nor, with their green and simple hue, disturb
The wild green landscape. Once again I see
These hedge-rows, hardly hedge-rows, little lines
Of sportive wood run wild; these pastoral farms
Green to the very door; and wreathes of smoke
Sent up, in silence, from among the trees,
With some uncertain notice, as might seem,
Of vagrant dwellers in the houseless woods,
Or of some hermit's cave, where by his fire
The hermit sits alone.

                    Though absent long,
These forms of beauty have not been to me,
As is a landscape to a blind man's eye:
But oft, in lonely rooms, and mid the din

---

* The river is not affected by the tides a few miles above Tintern.

Of towns and cities, I have owed to them,
In hours of weariness, sensations sweet,
Felt in the blood, and felt along the heart,
And passing even into my purer mind
With tranquil restoration: – feelings too
Of unremembered pleasure; such, perhaps,
As may have had no trivial influence
On that best portion of a good man's life;
His little, nameless, unremembered acts
Of kindness and of love. Nor less, I trust,
To them I may have owed another gift,
Of aspect more sublime; that blessed mood,
In which the burthen of the mystery,
In which the heavy and the weary weight
Of all this unintelligible world
Is lighten'd: – that serene and blessed mood,
In which the affections gently lead us on,
Until, the breath of this corporeal frame,
And even the motion of our human blood
Almost suspended, we are laid asleep
In body, and become a living soul:
While with an eye made quiet by the power
Of harmony, and the deep power of joy,
We see into the life of things.

                        If this
Be but a vain belief, yet, oh! how oft,
In darkness, and amid the many shapes
Of joyless day-light; when the fretful stir
Unprofitable, and the fever of the world,
Have hung upon the beatings of my heart,
How oft, in spirit, have I turned to thee
O sylvan Wye! Thou wanderer through the woods,
How often has my spirit turned to thee!

And now, with gleams of half-extinguish'd thought,
With many recognitions dim and faint,
And somewhat of a sad perplexity,
The picture of the mind revives again:
While here I stand, not only with the sense
Of present pleasure, but with pleasing thoughts
That in this moment there is life and food
For future years. And so I dare to hope
Though changed, no doubt, from what I was, when first
I came among these hills; when like a roe
I bounded o'er the mountains, by the sides
Of the deep rivers, and the lonely streams,
Wherever nature led; more like a man
Flying from something that he dreads, than one
Who sought the thing he loved. For nature then
(The coarser pleasures of my boyish days,
And their glad animal movements all gone by,)
To me was all in all. – I cannot paint
What then I was. The sounding cataract
Haunted me like a passion: the tall rock,
The mountain, and the deep and gloomy wood,
Their colours and their forms, were then to me
An appetite: a feeling and a love,
That had no need of a remoter charm,
By thought supplied, or any interest
Unborrowed from the eye. – That time is past,
And all its aching joys are now no more,
And all its dizzy raptures. Not for this
Faint I, nor mourn nor murmur: other gifts
Have followed, for such loss, I would believe,
Abundant recompence. For I have learned
To look on nature, not as in the hour
Of thoughtless youth, but hearing oftentimes
The still, sad music of humanity,
Not harsh nor grating, though of ample power

To chasten and subdue. And I have felt
A presence that disturbs me with the joy
Of elevated thoughts; a sense sublime
Of something far more deeply interfused,
Whose dwelling is the light of setting suns,
And the round ocean, and the living air,
And the blue sky, and in the mind of man,
A motion and a spirit, that impels
All thinking things, all objects of all thought,
And rolls through all things. Therefore am I still
A lover of the meadows and the woods,
And mountains; and of all that we behold
From this green earth; of all the mighty world
Of eye and ear, both what they half-create,*
And what perceive; well pleased to recognize
In nature and the language of the sense,
The anchor of my purest thoughts, the nurse,
The guide, the guardian of my heart, and soul
Of all my moral being.

              Nor, perchance,
If I were not thus taught, should I the more
Suffer my genial spirits to decay:
For thou art with me, here, upon the banks
Of this fair river; thou, my dearest Friend,
My dear, dear Friend, and in thy voice I catch
The language of my former heart, and read
My former pleasures in the shooting lights
Of thy wild eyes. Oh! yet a little while
May I behold in thee what I was once,
My dear, dear Sister! And this prayer I make,
Knowing that Nature never did betray

---

* This line has a close resemblance to an admirable line of Young, the exact
expression of which I cannot recollect.

The heart that loved her; 'tis her privilege,
Through all the years of this our life, to lead
From joy to joy: for she can so inform
The mind that is within us, so impress
With quietness and beauty, and so feed
With lofty thoughts, that neither evil tongues,
Rash judgments, nor the sneers of selfish men,
Nor greetings where no kindness is, nor all
The dreary intercourse of daily life,
Shall e'er prevail against us, or disturb
Our chearful faith that all which we behold
Is full of blessings. Therefore let the moon
Shine on thee in thy solitary walk;
And let the misty mountain winds be free
To blow against thee: and in after years,
When these wild ecstasies shall be matured
Into a sober pleasure, when thy mind
Shall be a mansion for all lovely forms,
Thy memory be as a dwelling-place
For all sweet sounds and harmonies; Oh! then,
If solitude, or fear, or pain, or grief,
Should be thy portion, with what healing thoughts
Of tender joy wilt thou remember me,
And these my exhortations! Nor, perchance,
If I should be, where I no more can hear
Thy voice, nor catch from thy wild eyes these gleams
Of past existence, wilt thou then forget
That on the banks of this delightful stream
We stood together; and that I, so long
A worshipper of Nature, hither came,
Unwearied in that service: rather say
With warmer love, oh! with far deeper zeal
Of holier love. Nor wilt thou then forget,
That after many wanderings, many years
Of absence, these steep woods and lofty cliffs,

And this green pastoral landscape, were to me
More dear, both for themselves, and for thy sake.

END

A NOTE ON THE TEXT

William Wordsworth (1770–1850) met Samuel Taylor Coleridge (1772–1834) in 1795. They became neighbours and then close friends in Somerset. They began to plan collaborative work, believing their imaginations to be in crucial ways complementary.

Lyrical Ballads was originally issued by Joseph Cottle, the bookseller, in Bristol in the summer of 1798, printed by William Pine. Cottle transferred the impression to the London booksellers J. and A. Arch, who published on 4 October. The review reception was slow and so were sales. By June 1800 the first edition had sold out. Longman paid £80 for the copyright in the second edition. It appeared with Wordsworth's name alone on the title page. The 1800 edition bears that date but did not appear until 1801.

The first edition differs substantially from the later, more familiar editions. Coleridge was responsible for four of the original poems: 'The Rime of the Ancyent Marinere', 'The Foster-Mother's Tale', 'The Nightingale' and 'The Dungeon'. The rest were by Wordsworth. Without Wordsworth's later, classic preface the critical apparatus was modest and the poems did not seem to exist as illustrations to justify an argument.

Joseph Cottle had published Coleridge's *Poems on Various Subjects* in April 1796. Coleridge sent him material piecemeal; Cottle provided an eventual fair copy which Coleridge further corrected, before proofs were issued; then Coleridge further revised in proof. Cottle played an important role in drawing together *Lyrical Ballads*. Coleridge originally offered him his and Wordsworth's tragedies, and a volume of Wordsworth's poems. Cottle visited Nether Stowey and seems to have proposed separate publication. But the poets wanted a joint volume, to be published anonymously. In April Coleridge told Cottle, 'We deem that the volumes offered to you are to a certain degree *one work, in kind tho' not in degree,* as an ode is one work; and that our different poems are as stanzas, good relatively rather than absolutely'. The letter shows how close (insofar as Coleridge speaks for both men) they were to notions of process rather than product, how 'romantic' their conception truly was. In May 1798 Wordsworth was in dire need of money. Coleridge could not complete all his pieces. Cottle paid 30 guineas for copyright in Wordsworth's poems. 'Tintern Abbey' was added when the book was being set in type.

Coleridge's poems in *Lyrical Ballads* were to treat 'supernatural, or at least romantic' subjects, while Wordsworth's were to treat ordinary subjects in order to 'excite a feeling analogous to the supernatural'. Wordsworth had hoped for collaboration in the actual composition, not only combination. He wrote the beginning of 'The Three Graves' for Coleridge to finish. Coleridge partly obliged but with his usual inability to bring things to a conclusion left it as a torso. 'The Ancyent Marinere' looks a little out of place as the only thoroughgoingly 'supernatural' piece. No wonder that in later editions Wordsworth moved it from the beginning to the middle of the book. Had he had his way, it would have been excluded altogether from later printings. In a letter to Cottle of 24 June 1799, Wordsworth wrote: 'From what I can gather it seems that The Ancyent Marinere has upon the whole been an injury to the volume, I mean that the old words and the strangeness of it have deterred readers from going on. If the volume should come to a second Edition I would put in its place some little things which would be more likely to suit the common taste.'

When Wordsworth published his complete poems in later life, he did not regard the *Lyrical Ballads* pieces as belonging together or forming a distinctive suite. He redistributed them throughout his *Poetical Works.* This is not surprising: the diversity of poems in 1798 *Lyrical Ballads* is haphazard, out of keeping with the programme announced in the 'Advertisement' which Wordsworth drafted, later elaborating it in his famous 'Preface' (1805).

Lyrical Ballads is almost an oxymoron: the lyric is an artful piece of writing, emphasizing sound organization, intended to express feeling or emotion; the ballad, in a common and even formulaic language, tells a tale, often in quatrains. In combining these terms the radical purpose of the two poets is established: a fusion which affects the language of 'literary' poetry but also the nature of narrative, imbuing it with 'emotion' line by line, as process, rather than in its final effects. What neither poet had in mind was 'music': the sung lyric and the sung ballad are remote from this volume.

In the later editions Wordsworth's forty-page Preface must have been at least as off-putting to a new reader as 'The Ancyent Marinere' had been in the first, a point Coleridge makes in *Biographia Literaria*. Charles Lamb thought the Preface should have been separately published: it over-stresses the experimental nature of poems 'sprung from living and daily circumstances' and as such 'associates a *diminishing* idea with the poems which follow'. The relative absence of 'poetic diction' in *Lyrical Ballads* is a radical response to conventions of the eighteenth century, deliberate strategy, not originality in the spirit of Burns, Blake or Smart. The title *Lyrical Ballads* announces to readers with Augustan expectations that distinct genres, lyric and ballad, are to be fused, in disregard of the rules.

'Ballad' misleads readers as to Wordsworth's attitude to the language of poetry. 'Ballad' suggests 'popular' verse in a popular idiom. But 'We Are Seven' was the only *Lyrical Ballad* published as a broadsheet. None has an especially dramatic narrative line. Narrative of action was never one of their special talents. The language avoids off-the-peg diction, it is a language men might *speak*: but they would hardly be likely to sing it. The poems address not the vulgar audience to which Burns appeals but the audience that read Crabbe and Cowper, the audience whose language Wordsworth, with a Cumberland accent, actually spoke. In *Lyrical Ballads* only Coleridge's 'The Ancyent Marinere' achieves consistent balladic effects.

Michael Schmidt